Catullus: A Sele

The following titles are available from Bloomsbury for the OCR specifications in Latin and Greek for examinations from June 2021 to June 2023

Catullus: A Selection of Poems, with introduction, commentary notes and vocabulary by John Godwin

Cicero *Pro Cluentio*: A Selection, with introduction, commentary notes and vocabulary by Matthew Barr

Livy *History of Rome* I: A Selection, with introduction, commentary notes and vocabulary by John Storey

Ovid *Heroides*: A Selection, with introduction, commentary notes and vocabulary by Christina Tsaknaki

Tacitus *Annals* IV: A Selection, with introduction, commentary notes and vocabulary by Robert Cromarty

Virgil *Aeneid* XII: A Selection, with introduction, commentary notes and vocabulary by James Burbidge

OCR Anthology for Classical Greek AS and A Level, covering the prescribed texts by Aristophanes, Homer, Plato, Plutarch, Sophocles and Thucydides, with introduction, commentary notes and vocabulary by Simon Allcock, Sam Baddeley, John Claughton, Alastair Harden, Sarah Harden, Carl Hope and Jo Lashly

Supplementary resources for these volumes can be found at
www.bloomsbury.com/OCR-editions-2021-2023
Please type the URL into your web browser and follow the instructions to access the Companion Website. If you experience any problems, please contact Bloomsbury at academicwebsite@bloomsbury.com

Catullus:
A Selection of Poems

Poems 1, 5, 6, 7, 8, 10, 11, 17, 34, 40, 62, 64 lines 124–264, 70, 76, 85, 88, 89, 91, 107

With introduction, commentary notes and
vocabulary by John Godwin

BLOOMSBURY ACADEMIC
LONDON • NEW YORK • OXFORD • NEW DELHI • SYDNEY

BLOOMSBURY ACADEMIC
Bloomsbury Publishing Plc
50 Bedford Square, London, WC1B 3DP, UK
1385 Broadway, New York, NY 10018, USA

BLOOMSBURY, BLOOMSBURY ACADEMIC and the Diana logo are
trademarks of Bloomsbury Publishing Plc

First published in Great Britain 2020

Cover design: Terry Woodley
Cover image © PHAS/UIG via Getty Images

A catalogue record for this book is available from the British Library.

A catalog record for this book is available from the Library of Congress.

ISBN: PB: 978-1-3500-6022-7
        ePDF: 978-1-3500-6024-1
        eBook: 978-1-3500-6023-4

Typeset by RefineCatch Limited, Bungay, Suffolk
Printed and bound in India

To find out more about our authors and books visit
www.bloomsbury.com and sign up for our newsletters.

Contents

Preface

The text and notes found in this volume are designed to guide any student who has mastered Latin up to GCSE level and wishes to read Catullus in the original.

The book, however, is particularly designed to support students who are reading Catullus' text in preparation for OCR's AS/A Level Latin examination in June 2022 and June 2023. (Please note that this edition uses 'AS' to refer indiscriminately both to AS itself and the first year of A Level, i.e. Group 3.)

This edition contains a detailed introduction to the historical and literary context of the poetry. The Commentary Notes to the text aim to help students to bridge the gap between GCSE and A Level Latin, and therefore focus on the harder points of grammar and word order as well as highlighting the literary and historical points of interest and making reference to other texts which are relevant to the poetry. I am aware that this book straddles both years of the A Level course, and so I have tried to write something which could be understood by a student fresh from GCSE while also giving something to students who are intending to pursue the subject to a higher level at university. At the end of the book is a full vocabulary list for all the words contained in the prescribed sections, with words in OCR's Defined Vocabulary List for AS Level Latin flagged by means of an asterisk.

My thanks are due above all to Alice Wright and her team at Bloomsbury, who have once again been a model of efficiency and enthusiasm. My thanks also go to Professor Susan Treggiari of Brasenose College, Oxford, for her expert help with the background to poem 62. I owe a huge debt of gratitude to Professor Stephen Heyworth of Wadham College, Oxford, to Dr Gail Trimble of Trinity College, Oxford, as well as to the anonymous OCR reader, who have all read this book, in whole or in part, and made many highly useful comments which saved me from error and pointed me towards a better reading of the text.

John Godwin
Shrewsbury, 2018

Introduction

Catullus and his world

Little is known about the life of Gaius Valerius Catullus. We are reasonably certain that his family must have been wealthy – if only because he clearly had such a good education at a time when education was not free – and we know also that his family came from Verona, a place he refers to in his poems (e.g. 68.27). He is recorded by St Jerome as living to the age of thirty, and Ovid (*Amores* III.9.61) tells us that he died young; and since there are no references in his poems to anything after 55 BC it is tempting to suggest that he was born in 84 BC and died in 54 BC. He seems to have climbed the ladder of political success (or at least scaled the lower rungs, as he mentions in poem 10 being on the staff of the praetor Gaius Memmius when he was governor of Bithynia in 57–56 BC) and he shows some interest in the personalities of the era such as Pompey, Caesar, Cicero and Clodius. The age he lived in was one of political upheaval as the old Roman Republic, in which competing aristocrats controlled the 'Senate and People of Rome', began to suffer body blows from the rising class of generals (who commanded the armies) and the orators (who swayed the law courts). The influx of slaves into Italy in the second century BC had led to a growing urban plebs, as smallholders sold their land and moved into the city. Caius Marius (157–86 BC) as consul and general had removed the property qualification required for military service and enlisted poor men into the legions in 106 BC; and ever since then, the troops had owed their loyalty to their general rather than to the state. This process of separating the military from the judicial and political power centres led swiftly to the dictatorship of Sulla (82–79 BC) and ultimately to the principate from 27 BC onwards. The exercise of power by army commanders generated mistrust, fear, anger and increased violence in the city – anger which is reflected in some of the poems of Catullus. He is, for instance, crudely insulting towards Pompey the Great (29), Julius Caesar (29, 54, 57, 93) and especially their henchman Mamurra (29, 94, 105, 114, 115). When Catullus fell foul of Julius Caesar, however, the great man forgave him and invited him to dinner (Suetonius *Julius Caesar* 73). The political engagement which we find in later poets such as Horace was a later phenomenon, born as he was into an age where the poet could enact the role of a prophetic voice (*vates*) and both reflect and possibly influence perceptions of political life. Catullus' poetry is closer to the *simplicitas* or 'outspoken bluntness' which Romans enjoyed, a bluntness employed and enjoyed by earlier satirists such as Lucilius.

Catullus enjoys mocking his contemporaries – such as Gellius, Furius, Aurelius, Varus, Piso – whom we can try to identify from other sources, along with others who elude identification, such as the hapless cuckold in 17. Flavius in poem 6 and Varus in 10 are mocked for their girlfriends, while Gellius is abused roundly for a catalogue of bad behaviour in poems 88–91. Other targets fare even worse in poems not included in this selection: the vilified girl Ameana, whose physical failings are listed, one by one, in poem 43, or the 'foul tart' with the 'face of a dog from Gaul', who has taken his writing tablets and refuses to return them in poem 42. Catullus' poems convey a power which can be directed for good or for ill, and he uses his verses as missiles more than once, such as in poem 40 where Ravidus is facing a firing squad of iambic lines. He is quick to mock others for (e.g.) their misuse of the letter 'h' (84), their bizarre dental hygiene (39), their choice of girlfriend (41 and also 6), their austere way of living (23), their disgusting lack of hygiene (97) and their sexual habits (poems 88–91). Catullus does not except himself from the mockery, of course, and shows himself in a far from flattering light when he attempts unsuccessfully to impress a girl in poem 10 or when he pleads with himself to stop loving a girl who clearly has stopped loving him (8, 11, 76). His poems show him as a lover who is randy (32), madly in love (51), romantic (5), disillusioned with his love affair (76) and even stuck with both love and hatred for the same person (85). We also see him playful with his friends (50), enthralled by a handsome young man (48) and bitterly jealous of anyone who tries to steal the youth from him (81). The poet gives us a sense of place, both rural – his beloved Sirmio on Lake Garda (31), and his estate in Tibur (44) – and also urban, as in the filthy bar of poem 37 or the street scene of poem 10.

Catullus and the 'New Poets'

Above all, Catullus gives us a sense of what it felt like to be alive in Rome in the first half of the first century BC, at around the same time as the didactic poet Lucretius and a generation before the Augustan poets: Virgil, the elegists Propertius and Tibullus, Horace, and (later still) Ovid. Catullus looked back at Greek literature such as the lyrics of Sappho (especially in poem 51, which is a translation of Sappho); he also made use of the frankness of the 'iambic' tradition in Greek verse of writers such as Hipponax (late sixth-century BC), whose characteristic metre (the 'scazon' or 'limping iambic') is used by Catullus in poem 8 (and seven other poems) and whose abusive and violent verses used words as weapons much as Catullus does in poems such as 40. The other great influence on Catullus' abusive verse was Archilochus (late seventh–sixth-century BC), whose range was wide but who also used verse both to recount his own experiences and to excoriate his enemies, some of whom allegedly hanged themselves in shame (see OCD s.v. 'Archilochus', 'Hipponax' and 'Iambic Poetry, Greek'). When we read Catullus lampooning Gellius (poems 88–91) or narrating his own sexual activities (56, 32), we could be listening to Archilochus.

The other great influence on Roman literature of this period was the work produced in the city of Alexandria in Egypt between about 280 and 240 BC. Here, a group of learned poets such as Theocritus, Apollonius and above all Callimachus created verse which was a new take on old themes, crafted and seeking formal perfection, avoiding the bombastic epic for the small scale and the intimate. Alexandrian poets gave their readers a new angle on mythological subjects and elevated the perfection of poetic craft above any moral or didactic message contained in the words – an aspiration towards 'art for art's sake'.

Catullus was not a lone voice in Roman poetry at the time. Other poets at the time of Catullus include such men as Calvus, Cinna, Cato and Cornificius, and of their works only fragments remain. Catullus and his colleagues are often termed the 'neoterics' or 'New Poets'. They all seem to have composed a similar range of poetry: epigrams, wedding songs, occasional verse in a variety of metres with erotic, obscene, humorous or satirical content. One poetic form favoured by these poets was the new form (in Latin) of the short epic or *epyllion* such as poem 64 of Catullus or the *Smyrna* of Cinna, the *Io* of Calvus, the *Glaucus* of Cornificius, the *Diana* of Valerius Cato and, perhaps, the *Magna Mater* of Caecilius (mentioned in poem 35). This sort of poem was minutely crafted in form (the *Smyrna* took nine years to write, according to Catullus (95.1–2)) and would be original in content, looking at a familiar story from an unfamiliar viewpoint: it might include additional myths, whether narrated (as in Callimachus' *Hecale*) or by means of an *ecphrasis* as in the Theseus and Ariadne 'digression' in Catullus poem 64. The subject matter was often love, especially 'pathological' love such as that of a girl for her father (*Smyrna*) or of a mortal for a sea-nymph (Catullus 64), or of a merman sea-god who fell for the nymph Scylla (*Glaucus*), or the mysterious world of Cybele as expounded by Caecilius (and in Catullus 63) – all the sort of stories which could be found in the Greek poet Parthenius' 'Sufferings of Love' (*Erotica pathemata*). The interest in erotic pathology which we find in these short epics (see, e.g., 64.132–201) is mirrored also in the psychological examination of love which we find in the short poems.

Short epics (such as poem 64) do not aim to tell the whole story, but rather expect the reader to know the whole story and to be able to appreciate the artistry of the poet who has sculpted what appears to be a miniature fragment of it in such unfragmentary perfection. This leads us on to another major Alexandrian feature: learning (*doctrina*). Alexandrian literature demands knowledge of history, geography and mythology and teases and flatters the reader with its arch allusive style: Catullus, who was later termed *doctus* by Ovid (*Amores* III.9.63) and Martial (I.61.1, 14.100), alludes to such things as literary history (e.g. *Battiades* 116.2), geography (4.6–15, 7.4, 11.5–12), mythology (e.g. 64, *Thyonianus* in 27.7, Tethys in 88). More striking still is the poet's use of contrasting themes (faithful friends vs unfaithful woman, for instance, in 11) and his interest in the bizarre (90), the obscure (66), the unexpected (the shifts of feeling and perspective in 8, the self-mockery in 10). He concentrates on the poems as things in themselves, which can wound (12.10–11, 40.2), or bless with immortality (6.16–17), or curse with notoriety (40), and whose creation can render the poet sleepless with excitement (50) and the reader mad with lust (35). It is worth lingering over the poems in which Catullus speaks of poetry itself to develop a picture of his notion of the importance and the aesthetics of his craft, and of his interaction with other poets.

Many literary 'groups' define themselves negatively by contrasting their own practice with that of other (inferior) writers – as Callimachus famously did in his influential preface to the *Aitia*. Catullus defines the 'good poetry' of himself and his friends primarily by contrast to the 'poor poetry' of long-winded, bombastic epic – the sort of verse which (he claims) was turned out by the yard by inferior poets with no talent except stamina. He calls the *Annals* of Volusius toilet paper (*cacata carta*, 'shitty sheets', 36.1, 20) and fish paper (literally 'loose tunics for mackerel', 95.8). This poem (36) damns Volusius by example as well as by execration: Catullus' learned religious references are a world away from the laboured poetry of Volusius which is (he says) 'full of the countryside' (36.19), and Catullus is (as it were) showing off how Volusius *should* be writing. Suffenus is similarly derided in poem 22 for the elegant (and expensive) appearance of his book which conceals the 'rustic' contents which are prodigiously long: another waste of good money and paper (although the ending of this poem is interestingly modest and rather reduces the polemical tone). A parcel of such bad poetry is seen in poem 14 as deserving a counter-blast both in the poem itself and in a return parcel of named bad poets.

In poem 50, we see the poet recalling a session of poetry-writing with Calvus, and the emphasis throughout is on the contrast between the 'lightness' (*versiculos*, 4) and 'playfulness' (*lusimus*, 2) of the verse and the serious effects it had on the poet, whose passionate response (*dolorem*, 17) is one more appropriate to a lover. This sort of verse may be 'slender' and light, but that does not mean it is not to be taken seriously – quite the reverse, for all the poet's self-effacing talk of 'trifling efforts' (*nugas* 1.4). Poetry is called for when in a depressed state (38) or is needed to punish the wrongdoer (40, 42). Poem 35 is a brilliant combination of the 'invitation' poem, with praise of Caecilius' success with a girl and also of his poetry: Caecilius is called a *poeta tener* ('love-poet') who writes 'elegantly' (*venuste*) – and so inspires love (of which Venus was the goddess) in his female readers. The contrast of the slender elegant miniature epic (which will travel far and live long) with the flatulent epic of lesser poets (which will get no further than the local river and end up wrapping mackerel) is made explicit in poem 95, where Cinna's *Smyrna* is contrasted with (again) Volusius' *Annales*. Interestingly, the poem also contrasts the new Latin poetry with Greek poetry of several centuries before: Antimachus, whose poem *Lyde* was described by Callimachus (fr. 398Pf.) as 'fat and inelegant', is said by Catullus to be 'swollen' (*tumido*), showing that Callimachus' opinion on Antimachus was copied, word for word, by Catullus and applied to the poetry of his own day.

This contrast of the elegant literature of a Callimachus and the boorish alternative is the note on which our collection ends (poem 116), as Catullus expresses his determination to use the weapons of fine words rather than throw pearls before swine. The collection (and perhaps one of Catullus' original books) thus closes with a further affirmation of the Callimachean literary values of elegance, wit, grace, brevity and charm, with which poem 1 begins. We are left with the impression that Catullus formed a bond of solidarity with other poets of like mind (*sodalis* 95.9) and they established a bond of hostility towards poets who did not share their Alexandrian love of the exquisite miniature.

Lesbia – the life of love

Catullus' poetry is thus learned, clever and ironic – but it is not removed from real life. Readers, throughout the centuries, have been moved by the feelings and the passion of the lines, and the undoubted artistry of the poet is put to good use in expressing what are powerful human emotions and the range of human experience. The poems addressed to 'Lesbia', in particular, have been found so moving that scholars since antiquity have wanted to identify the woman in question.

Whatever her real name, it was not 'Lesbia', which was clearly a light pseudonym and establishes a clear link with Sappho, the most famous woman poet in antiquity and a native of Lesbos. Catullus translated some verses of Sappho into Latin in poem 51, keeping both the meaning of the words and also the metre of the original, and at least one scholar (Quinn) has suggested that this may have been his first poem to her and given rise to the private name which they used to disguise her real name. A later writer (Apuleius *Apology* 10) tells us that her real name was Clodia, an identification which is made more secure by poem 79, where Clodius is given the nickname 'Lesbius'. She has often been identified more closely as Clodia Metelli, the wife of Quintus Metellus Celer and the sister of the populist politician Clodius, and this makes for a temptingly neat storyline. Her husband was conveniently absent from Rome in 62 BC as a governor of Cisalpine Gaul, and Clodia allegedly misbehaved while he was away: when he died in 59 BC, there were people who suggested she may have poisoned him as it was in that year that she took up with Caelius Rufus. When Caelius ended their affair in 56, this scorned woman made up the allegation that her former lover had poisoned her late husband, hoping to kill two birds with one stone, only for her to be demolished by the oratory of

Cicero's *Pro Caelio*. Catullus' Lesbia was married at the time of their affair (68.146, 83.1), and we can be sure that 'Lesbius' in 79 refers to a Clodius because the opening sentence runs *Lesbius est pulcher*, and *pulcher* ('handsome') was the cognomen of (among others) Publius Clodius Pulcher, a pun also made much of by Cicero (e.g. *Letters to Atticus* 2.1.4).

The story is good but the facts remains hazy, not least because there are probably several different girls in these poems – the young girl playing with a sparrow in poems 2 and 3 does not sound like the *femme fatale* of poem 11, for instance. The historical 'Lesbia' is, of course, of secondary interest – on a par with Shakespeare's 'dark lady' in the *Sonnets* – since what matters most in the analysis and enjoyment of the text is the poetry itself and the ways in which it portrays aspects of human emotion and behaviour, crystallised into verse of enduring appeal. There are the happy moments of apparent joy (as in poems 5, 7, 68, 70, 109), along with the boastful poems about her superiority to other women (43, 86), and then the poems of disillusion when the poet is betrayed by her infidelities (11, 58) and the ones which chart the confused feelings of this heartbroken lover (72, 76, 85, 104). Sometimes, these poems are set side by side (such as poems 7 and 8), in a kaleidoscopic array of moods.

Not that this poet presents himself as a model of fidelity and chastity. He invites the sexually adept Ipsitilla to visit him for sex (32) and addresses passionate poems to and about a young man called Iuventius, whose 'honeyed eyes' the poet would love to kiss hundreds of thousands of times (poem 48) and whom the poet wishes to keep from his priapic friends (15, 21, 24). The banter surrounding the sex lives of the poet and his friends finds ready expression here, from a Flavius ashamed of his 'tart' (6) to a Varus whose girl embarrasses the poet (10). Less appealing perhaps, but equally memorable, are the poems of obscene invective directed at the sex lives of others such as Vibennius and his son (33), Rufa (59), Gellius (74, 80, 88–91), Naso (112), Maecilia (113), Aufillena (110), Mamurra (57, 94).

Catullus' poetry

Poetry, of course, is not just versified diaries, and we have to be cautious about mapping the life of the poet from his art – as Catullus bluntly tells his friends Furius and Aurelius in poem 16 ('the poet ought to be pure in his personal life, but there is no need for his poems to be pure', 5–6). All the poetry in this book – even the most apparently artless – is, in fact, cleverly composed and expressed, as the commentary seeks to make clear.

This artistry is most obvious in the longer poems (61–8). Poem 64, for instance, at 406 lines, is by far the longest poem in the collection and gives us a magical evocation of the wedding of the mortal Peleus and the sea-nymph Thetis after their surprise encounter in mid-ocean. The wedding is arranged and the marriage bed is described; the illustrations on its coverlet allow the poet to indulge in a descriptive 'digression' (*ecphrasis*) longer than the surrounding narrative, an account of the abandoning of Ariadne by her faithless lover Theseus on the island of Naxos. The shock value of this is enormous – not only the formal shock of having a 'digression' which exceeds the framing narrative, but also the tasteless nerve to show such a testament to male faithlessness at a wedding celebrating romantic love. Shocking, too, is the prophecy of the Fates who sing the wedding song: where we might expect the chorus of Muses, we have three old ladies with white hair and almost toothless mouths singing of the future offspring of Peleus and Thetis, the great Greek hero Achilles. To be told that one's child will grow into a great hero is one thing, but Peleus and Thetis are told that he will mow down his enemies like grass, choke the stream of the river Scamander with heaps of slain bodies and have a young girl sacrificed on his tomb – all of which are unusual elements in a wedding song. The poem is held together by themes, and one of these is the key idea of gods mingling with humans, as seen in Peleus (mortal) marrying Thetis (immortal) and also Ariadne (mortal) meeting Bacchus (immortal): the poem ends with a moralising epilogue, whose ostensible purpose is to explain why it is that such mixed marriages of mortals and gods no longer happen because of human wickedness repelling the gods, but whose language also hints that the heroic age (with its fratricide, 150, 399, for instance) was perhaps no better than our own.

Poem 64, then, is a surprising poem in many ways. We constantly find our expectations foiled by the poet. It starts out sounding like another Medea story – with strong echoes of earlier accounts of the Medea tale – but it is not. We then think it is a poem about the voyage of the Argo – the first ship to sail and the vessel which would most plausibly introduce mariners to sea-nymphs – but (again) it is not. It turns out to be about a wedding.

The wedding is interrupted by the lengthy description of the coverlet which shifts the optimism of the wedding to the pessimism of love betrayed, only to shift the despair of Ariadne with the prospect of her salvation at the hands of her divine lover Dionysus. The future of Achilles is glorious and also disturbing, while the outlook for 'us' (*nobis* 406) is bleak and godless. The poem has immense variety of scene and mood and, above all, the poem is a kaleidoscope of poetic and sensuous pleasure.

Poem 63 is an equally shocking account of the self-castration of the youth Attis when he is in a state of religious frenzy, worshipping the 'Great Mother' Cybele: here again, the poet invests so much feeling into the poem that some scholars have seen it as, in some ways, allegorical of Catullus' own emasculation at the hands of his beloved.

The two wedding hymns (61 and 62) differ in the degree to which they relate to Roman weddings, while poem 65 dedicates to Hortalus the following piece (66), which is a translation of a poem by the highly influential Greek poet Callimachus about the turning of a lock of royal hair belonging to the Egyptian queen Berenice into a constellation in the heavens. There then follows a wonderfully scabrous tale of lurid gossip: poem 67 is a dialogue between the poet and a door which is encouraged to tell the scurrilous stories to which it has access – in this case, a tale of impotence and adultery which would do justice to the nastiest Twitter-feed.

The last of the 'long poems' (68, although this text is probably two separate poems joined together) is sublime and is perhaps the best poem which this poet ever created. It also typifies his work, in that it blends the personal and the mythological, romance and tragedy. The 'setting' is the poet's love-making with his married lover, but the 'gleaming goddess' (*candida diva* 68.70) is never described except in terms of her effect on the poet and her married status (135–46). The relationship of the poet and his mistress reminds him of the love of Protesilaus and Laudamia, a love which was doomed to frustration when Protesilaus was killed in the Trojan War. This then reminds him of the death of his brother, who has died in Northern Turkey, close to the site of ancient Troy. Weaving these themes – of Catullus, his brother and the legend of Troy and of history and family, love and grief – the poet creates a web of poetic analogy which relies heavily on the device of the simile. This poem, in fact, uses the simile to such an extent that there are more lines of simile than there are of 'straight' narrative, and again the effect is one of dazzling poetic pleasure, whereby the male poet is equated to the female lover Laodamia. The poem is constructed in a form of ring composition and shows beyond all doubt that poetry for Catullus is born of hard work and detailed planning rather than any mere outpouring of instant emotion. The feelings are channelled through lines of metrical and linguistic sophistication which link past and present, sorrow and joy, beauty and the repellent ugliness of death.

This superb poetic ability in the long poems is matched on a small scale in the shorter works but is also contrasted with some shocking obscenity in these texts. The criticism meted out to him that he must be a louche individual because he writes 'naughty verses' prompts him to compose a spirited defence (poem 16) of the writer against the 'documentary fallacy' and the poem's famous obscenity is there for rhetorical effects. His critics think that a poet of soft romantic poet verses (16.4) is less of a man and so this poet threatens homosexual rape of two kinds to assert his masculine superiority over them.

Catullus' choice of this sort of language has over the years raised eyebrows and led some to judge that his quality as a poet is uneven when he descends to the level of language more often seen as graffiti than as great art. The 'rude' poems of Catullus have certainly earned him a great deal of notoriety and some people find it hard to cope with the shift in tone and style when we read a poem of high emotion and depth such as his lament for the death of his friend's wife (96), side by side with one of the most obscene poems in any language (97), whose purpose is to mock a certain malodorous Aemilius. Catullus – like Horace, who can also raise eyebrows – is a poet of many parts and many moods: he also sees no reason why any words in the dictionary should be barred from poetry. A good poet can perform the alchemy of turning the unclean into the pure gold of poetry. The ancient attitude towards the sexual and the scatological is, of course, different from our own: the reader of Aristophanic comedy (which predates Catullus by about four centuries) or Juvenalian satire (composed in the early second century AD) will recognise Catullus' obscenity as part of a long and vigorous tradition of elegant verbal abuse, the words used very much as weapons in a war of personal attack as well as in a celebration of life at its most exuberant.

Catullus managed to create some of the most memorable and influential verses which the Romans ever produced. Later writers recognised the famous 'sparrow' poem and even did it the honour of imitating it, as, for instance, Ovid did when he created a lament for the death of his girlfriend's parrot (*Amores* II.6). The poems of Catullus, above all, impart the feeling that poetry matters: it is a worthwhile way to spend one's time and can even rob the poet of sleep (50). It demands everything (it is difficult for the poet to produce verse if his heart is in turmoil, 68.1–14) and can change lives. Poetry can fire insults at people who deserve it (e.g. 29, 88–9) and can also express feelings of tenderness in language of great elegance and sensitivity (3, 9, 11.21–4, 48, 62.39–58).

Some literary and linguistic terms used in the Commentary

a fortiori refers to the 'all the more' line of argument ('x is bigger than y and y is bigger than z so, *a fortiori*, x is bigger than z'): see 76.18 and introduction to poem 11.

alliteration is repetition of consonants (e.g. 6.7 *cubile clamat*, 64.146 *promittere parcunt*).

amoebean is a style of composition where two voices alternate and compete with one another, as in poem 62.

anaphora is the emphatic repetition of a word in successive phrases such as 62.15, 62.44, 64.186–7.

apo koinou (a Greek term: ἀπὸ κοινοῦ) denotes the form of phrase, where a single word functions in two separate clauses, as in 107.3.

apodosis is the other half of a conditional from the 'if' clause or protasis: so, at 6.13, 'you would not be showing' (*non pandas*) is the apodosis, while *ni . . . facias* ('if you were not doing') is the protasis.

apostrophe is where the narrator addresses a character in the story in the second person, e.g. 64.253.

assonance is the repetition of vowel sounds, as in 8.8 *fulsērĕ vērē*.

asyndeton is the omission of connective words such as 'and': see, e.g., 8.11 *perfer, obdura*.

bathos is the effect achieved where a 'high' and lofty tone suddenly gives way to brutal and low terms: see, e.g., poem 11 and poem 88.5–8.

chiasmus is the use of A–B–B–A pattern in sounds, ideas and words: see, e.g., 62.21–2 (*natam – matris – matris – natam*), 64.141, 152–3.

cognate accusative denotes a word in the accusative which is the object of the verb which has the same meaning and the same root, as in 7.9 (*basia basiare*).

compound adjectives are formed of more than one word joined together into a single adjective: e.g. 7.4 *lasarpiciferis*.

correlatives connect parallel phrases with terms such as *qualis . . . talis*, or *quantus . . . tantus* as in 64.200–1.

diminutives are forms of words which suggest a small version of the simple word, usually by adding a suffix. The diminutive of *liber* (book) is *libellus* (1.1): cf. 6.3 (*scortillum*), 17.3 (*ponticuli*).

ecphrasis denotes a digression which pauses the action of the narrative to describe a scene or a work of art, such as the lengthy description of the coverlet of the marriage bed at 64.50–264.

enactment is where the words somehow replicate verbally the scene being described, such as the repetition of words (*mille deinde centum, dein mille . . . dein . . . centum . . .*) indicating a repeated succession of kisses at 5.7–10.

enjambement is the emphatic leaving of the last word of a phrase or sentence to the start of the following line of verse, as at 10.27 (*deferri*), 64.137 (*consilium*), 64.150 (*eripui*).

epanalepsis is the repetition of a word in a subsequent clause, as 17.14–15 (*puella / et puella . . .*), 64.259–60 (*orgia cistis / orgia . . .*).

epyllion is a miniature epic poem, often dealing with an unfamiliar tale or an unfamiliar aspect of a well-known tale; see the introductory paragraphs to poem 64.

gnomic refers either to a generalised statement (e.g. 62.16) or else to the use of the perfect tense to indicate a general rule for all time (e.g. 62.42, 64.148 (*metuere*)).

golden line refers to a line of hexameter verse which has the 'abVAB' pattern: adjective a – adjective b – verb – noun a – noun b. See, e.g., 64.129, 163, 172, 242, 264.

hendiadys is when a single idea is presented as if it were two separate things: e.g. 76.20 (*pestem perniciemque*).

hiatus denotes a passage where a word ending with a vowel precedes a word beginning with a vowel but where there is no elision as expected: see, e.g., 107.1.

hypallage is 'transferred epithet' such as 6.10–11 (*quassa* really goes with the bed, not with the *argutatio*).

hyperbaton is the deliberate placing of words outside where they are expected to be: *tam* in 6.13, *neque quod* at 91.5.

hyperbole is exaggeration for rhetorical or comic effect, as at 11.18–20, 17.14–16, 62.46.

implicit myth refers to a use of words which suggests reference to a mythical tale without explicitly naming it: 62.7.

juxtaposition is the placing of words next to each other for effect: e.g. 5.3 (*omnes unius*), 11.17 (*vivat valeatque*).

litotes is understatement such as when 'not bad' means 'good'.
See, e.g., 6.6 (*non viduas* ('not single'), 10.4 (*non sane illepidum*
(= *lepidum*)).

metaphor describes one thing in terms of another: 8.3 (*soles* to
denote happy days), 17.19 (*suppernata*), 62.46 (the flower of
virginity).

metonymy is a use of words referring to something with words
associated with it: e.g. 64.128 ('salt' for the sea), 64.162 ('footsteps'
for 'feet'). See also *synecdoche*.

onomatopeia is where the sound of words imitates the thing being
described: 11.4 (*tunditur unda* of the crashing waves), 64.258
(snakes described with sibilant sounds), 64.261–4.

partitive genitive is the use of the genitive case with words indicating
'some of', 'all of' and the like: e.g. 1.8, 5.13.

pathetic fallacy endows inanimate things with human feelings: see,
e.g., 64.179 (*truculentum*).

pejorative words seek to impart a damning opinion of the thing being
described: 6.4–5 (*febriculosi scorti*), 10.33 (*insulsa*).

polysyndeton is excessive use of connective words such as *et* or *-que*:
17.9 (*per caputque pedesque*), 64.201 (*seque suosque*).

protasis – see **apodosis**.

rhetorical questions usually do not expect to be answered and are
posed for emphasis: 8.15–18, 64.132–8.

ring composition denotes the shaping of a text so that the ending
recalls the beginning such as in poems 8 and 76.

similes describe one thing as being like another: poem 7 has two such
similes comparing the number of kisses with the number of grains
of sand (7.3–6) and stars in the sky (7.7–8), while poem 17
compares the dolt of a husband to a lump of wood (17.18–19).

synecdoche uses the word for a part of a thing to refer to the whole
thing: e.g. 'poopdecks' means 'ships' at 64.172.

tricolon crescendo is a series of three phrases, each one longer
than the one before, often all beginning with the same word, as
at 64.156.

The metres

Latin poetry from Plautus onwards was composed in imitation of Greek verse, in formal rhythmic patterns, in which the weight of syllables (as either heavy or light) was the determinant of the rhythm of the verse, rather than the natural stresses of the words as in English. Syllables were light (marked ∪ in this book) if the vowel was short and not followed by two (or more) consonants, whereas syllables containing long vowels, or diphthongs, or cases where a vowel was followed by a succession of consonants, were heavy (–). For example, the diphthong (double vowel) *ae* in *caelum* makes the first syllable of that word heavy in 6.17, and the short vowel *et* still produces a heavy syllable in 76.25 because it is followed by the initial consonant of *taetrum*. When a vowel (or a vowel +*m* as in the word *divum* in 76.4) ended a word and another vowel started the next word, the two syllables were usually crushed together in what is called 'elision', so that the three syllables of *divum ad* was read as two syllables *div(um) ad* and the two words *numine abusum* (76.4) would be read *numin(e) abusum*.

The poems in this volume are composed in a variety of metres, as follows:

Poems 62 and 64 were composed in the epic **hexameter** metre. The line is divided into six 'feet', each of which is either a dactyl (a heavy syllable followed by two light syllables (–∪∪ in conventional notation)) or a spondee (two heavy syllables (– –)). The last foot is always one of two syllables, and the last syllable of all may be either heavy or light (in which case, it is marked with the symbol '×'). The metrical analysis of a line is called 'scansion' and a typical hexameter line (64.144) may be scanned thus:

– ∪ ∪| –   – |– / – | – – |– ∪ ∪|– –
nūllă vĭ|rī spēr|ēt/sēr|mōnēs| ēssĕ fĭd|ēlēs

where the / sign shows the 'caesura' – the word break in the middle of a foot – which usually occurs in the third foot. The final two feet of the line usually allow the normal speech accent of the words to match the metrical 'downbeat' (ictus) thus, where the speech accent is marked in bold:

ac tum| praerup|tos/ tris|tem cons|cendere |montes (64.126)

Where there is no caesura, this does not occur and causes the rhythm of the end of the line to be odd (e.g. 62.45, 64.141). Poems 65–116 are composed in **elegiac** couplets, where hexameter lines (as above) alternate with 'pentameter' lines. The pentameter is made up of five feet but the line is always scanned in two halves of 2.5 feet. The feet are (as in hexameters) made up of dactyls or (in the first half of the line) spondees but the central pause or caesura is invariable and marks the division of the line into its two constituent halves. Occasionally, there is elision of the final syllable before the mid-point (e.g. *Nymphar(um) abluat* at 88.6). The final single syllable may be either heavy or light.

76.12, for instance, breaks down as follows:

$$- \ -| - \ -|- \ / -\cup\cup| - \ \cup \ \cup| \times$$
ēt dīs| īnvīt| īs/ dēsǐnǐs| ēssě mǐ|sěr

The first sixty-one poems are written in a variety of rhythms. Those found in the poems in this book are as follows:

Hendecasyllabics are lines of eleven syllables in the form:

$$- \ - \ - \ \cup\cup - \cup - \cup - \times$$

although, in some poems, the first two syllables are flexible and may be — $\cup$ (as at 1.2, 8, 9) or $\cup$ — (as at 1.4, 40.2).

So, for instance, the opening line of poem 1 reads:

cuī dōnō lěpǐdūm nǒvūm lǐbēllǔm

Poem 11 is composed in **Sapphic stanzas**, a metre of four-line units:

$$- \cup - \times - \cup\cup - \cup - -$$
$$- \cup - \times - \cup\cup - \cup - -$$
$$- \cup - \times - \cup\cup - \cup - -$$
$$- \cup\cup - \times$$

Fūr[i] ĕt Aūrēlī cŏmĭtēs Cătūllī,
sīv[e] ĭn ēxtrēmōs pĕnĕtrābĭt Īndōs,
lītŭs ūt lōngē rĕsŏnānt[e] Ēōā
tūndĭtŭr ūndā

Poem 8 is written in 'limping iambics' or '**scazons**', where the
normal ∪— rhythm of the iambic metre is inverted in the last pair
of syllables to become —∪, thus:

Mĭsēr| Cătūl||lĕ, dēs|ĭnās| ĭnēp|tīrĕ

Poem 17 is composed in a metre known as '**priapeans**', in which
a glyconic phrase (× ×/ —∪∪—/∪—) is followed by a pherecratean
(× ×/ — ∪∪ — / —) thus:

ō Cŏ|lōnĭă, quāe| cŭpīs/pōntĕ| lūdĕrĕ lōng|ō.

Poem 34 is metrically similar to poem 17, consisting of four-line
stanzas, in which three glyconics are followed by a final pherecratean:

ō Lātōnĭă, māxĭmī
māgnă prōgĕnĭēs Iŏvīs,
quăm mātēr prŏpĕ Dēlĭăm
dēpŏsīvĭt ŏlīvăm.

The transmission of the text

This is primarily an edition for sixth-formers and there is no need for
a lengthy account of the manuscripts, but it is worth reminding
readers that we are fortunate to be able to read this poetry at all.
Although poem 1 shows that Catullus gathered together at least some
of his poems, we do not have coherent books such as we find for the
Augustan poets.

Early circulation will have been on papyrus rolls, perhaps three of
them in a posthumous gathering together of much of his work. Until
the introduction of printing in the fifteenth century, all substantial

copies were made by scribes writing out, line by line, what they saw in the manuscript in front of them. Because the tradition relies on a single manuscript tradition, there are many places where the reading is dubious – we all make mistakes when transcribing other people's handwriting and copies of copies simply add more mistakes as copyists add their own errors to ones already there.

The earliest extant manuscript of Catullus is an anthology of poetry from the ninth century; this contains just poem 62. It shares with the later 'complete' manuscripts errors such as the gap after 62.32. There are increasing signs of knowledge of the poems from the late thirteenth century on, and we have three copies written in Italy in the second half of the fourteenth century. Derived from these are the many fifteenth-century manuscripts and the printed editions (from 1472). By this time, there were over a thousand textual flaws, and many of them (such as 1.9 and 10.26) remain unsolved to this day, while others (e.g. 11.11–12) continue to divide scholars. 64.243, where the anxious father Aegeus sees the black sails on his son's ship as he returns home, is a good case in point: the manuscript tradition reads *inflati lintea veli* ('sheets of billowing sail') but the word *inflati* seemed too banal to some and Sabellicus, in 1495, suggested *infecti* ('darkened') as a better word to describe the dark-coloured sail. I have printed the Sabellicus reading but cannot easily dismiss the manuscript reading. Catullus has made it quite clear what colour the sails are, and 'billowing' shows us the sails proclaiming the bad news while keeping the theme of strong winds from lines 239–40. A quick straw poll of editors shows the field evenly divided between the two readings.

Textual criticism is always based on a sensitive reading of the poetry, and sometimes the inspired insight of the critic enhances the poetry: a good example is 64.282, where the manuscript reads *aurea perit flores*, which is nonsense. *aurea* was quickly emended to *aura* and *parit* written for *perit* ('the breeze gives birth to flowers') but it took the poetic genius of A. E. Housman to see that *perit* points to an original *aperit*, giving us the sublime image of the warm breeze 'opening the flowers'.

In the five-and-a-half centuries since the first printed, text Catullus has never lacked readers and admirers. The continuing process of defining exactly what the poet first wrote is one which is inspired, above all, by admiration and love for the work which he produced.

Abbreviations

AG   Allen, J. H. and Greenough, J. B., *New Latin Grammar*

OCD   *The Oxford Classical Dictionary*

OLD   *The Oxford Latin Dictionary*

Editions of Catullus include

Ellis, Robinson (1889) Oxford (text and commentary in separate volumes).
Fordyce, C. J. (1961) Oxford: Oxford University Press (text and commentary: omits 88).
Garrison, D. H. (1989) *The Student's Catullus*, London: Routledge (text and commentary).
Godwin, J. (1995) Catullus: *Poems 61–68*, Warminster: Aris and Phillips (text with facing translation and commentary).
Godwin, J. (1999) Catullus: *The Shorter Poems*, Warminster: Aris and Phillips (text with facing translation and commentary).
Quinn, K. (1970) London: Macmillan (text and commentary).
Thomson, D. F. S. (1997) Toronto: University of Toronto Press (text and commentary).

Translations of Catullus include

Goold, G. P. (1989) *Catullus*, London: Duckworth.
Green, P. (2007) *The Poems of Catullus: A Bilingual Edition*, Berkeley and Los Angeles, CA: University of California Press.
Lee, G. (2008) *Catullus: The Complete Poems*, Oxford: Oxford University Press.

Books about Catullus include

Du Quesnay, I. and Woodman, A. (2012) *Catullus: Poems, Books, Readers,*
Cambridge: Cambridge University Press, esp. chapters 1–4.

Fitzgerald, W. (1995) *Catullan Provocations: Lyric Poetry and the Drama
of Position*, Berkeley, CA: University of California Press.

Godwin, J. (2008) *Reading Catullus*, Liverpool: Liverpool University
Press.

Hurley, A. K. (2004) *Catullus*, Bristol: Bristol Classical Press.

Jenkyns, R. (1982) *Three Classical Poets*, London: Duckworth, 85–150.

Quinn, K. (1959) *The Catullan Revolution*, Cambridge: Cambridge
University Press.

Wiseman, T. P. (1974) *Cinna the Poet and Other Roman Essays*, Leicester:
Leicester University Press.

Wiseman, T. P. (1985) *Catullus and His World*, Cambridge: Cambridge
University Press.

Wray, D. (2001) *Catullus and the Poetics of Roman Manhood*, Cambridge:
Cambridge University Press.

On the Neoteric Poets

Lyne, R. O. A. M. (1978) 'The Neoteric Poets', *Classical Quarterly*, 28:
167–87.

On the use of sexual terminology

Adams, J. N. (1982) *The Latin Sexual Vocabulary*, London: Duckworth.

On the context of poem 62 and
Roman Marriage generally

Treggiari, S. (1991) *Roman Marriage*, Oxford: Oxford University Press.

Useful collections of articles on Catullus include

Gaisser, J.H. (ed.) (2007) *Catullus*, Oxford Readings in Classical Studies, Oxford: Oxford University Press.

Skinner, M. B. (ed.) (2007) *A Companion to Catullus*, Blackwell Companions to the Ancient World, Oxford: Wiley-Blackwell.

For more on the metre see

Raven, D. S. (1998) *Latin Metre*, London: Bloomsbury.

For more on the text of Catullus see

Kiss, D. (ed.) (2015) *What Catullus Wrote: Problems in Textual Criticism, Editing and the Manuscript Tradition*, Swansea: Classical Press of Wales.

McKie, D. S. (2009) *Essays in the Interpretation of Roman Poetry*, Cambridge: Cambridge Classical Press.

Trappes-Lomaz, J. M. (2007) *Catullus: A Textual Reappraisal*, Swansea: Classical Press of Wales.

See also the very useful website of Kiss, containing a text, a full apparatus and images of three key manuscripts, available at: http://catullusonline. org/CatullusOnline/index.php.

For suggestions for further reading on each poem, see the webpages accompanying this book.

Text

1

cui dono lepidum novum libellum
arida modo pumice expolitum?
Corneli, tibi: namque tu solebas
meas esse aliquid putare nugas.
iam tum, cum ausus es unus Italorum   5
omne aevum tribus explicare cartis,
doctis, Iuppiter, et laboriosis!
quare habe tibi quidquid hoc libelli –
qualecumque, quod, o patrona virgo,
plus uno maneat perenne saeclo!   10

5

vivamus mea Lesbia, atque amemus,
rumoresque senum severiorum
omnes unius aestimemus assis!
soles occidere et redire possunt:
nobis cum semel occidit brevis lux,   5
nox est perpetua una dormienda.
da mi basia mille, deinde centum,
dein mille altera, dein secunda centum,
deinde usque altera mille, deinde centum.
dein, cum milia multa fecerimus,   10
conturbabimus illa, ne sciamus,
aut ne quis malus invidere possit,
cum tantum sciat esse basiorum.

6

Flavi, delicias tuas Catullo,
ni sint illepidae atque inelegantes,
velles dicere nec tacere posses.
verum nescioquid febriculosi
scorti diligis: hoc pudet fateri.   5
nam te non viduas iacere noctes
nequiquam tacitum cubile clamat
sertis ac Syrio fragrans olivo,
pulvinusque peraeque et hic et illic
attritus, tremulique quassa lecti   10
argutatio inambulatioque.
nam nil stare valet, nihil tacere.
cur? non tam latera ecfututa pandas,
ni tu quid facias ineptiarum.
quare, quidquid habes boni malique,   15

AS

dic nobis. volo te ac tuos amores
ad caelum lepido vocare versu.

7

quaeris, quot mihi basiationes
tuae, Lesbia, sint satis superque.
quam magnus numerus Libyssae harenae
lasarpiciferis iacet Cyrenis
oraclum Iovis inter aestuosi   5
et Batti veteris sacrum sepulcrum;
aut quam sidera multa, cum tacet nox,
furtivos hominum vident amores:
tam te basia multa basiare
vesano satis et super Catullo est,   10
quae nec pernumerare curiosi
possint nec mala fascinare lingua.

8

miser Catulle, desinas ineptire,
et quod vides perisse perditum ducas.
fulsere quondam candidi tibi soles,
cum ventitabas quo puella ducebat
amata nobis quantum amabitur nulla.   5
ibi illa multa cum iocosa fiebant,
quae tu volebas nec puella nolebat,
fulsere vere candidi tibi soles.
nunc iam illa non vult: tu quoque impotens noli,
nec quae fugit sectare, nec miser vive,   10
sed obstinata mente perfer, obdura.
vale puella, iam Catullus obdurat,

nec te requiret nec rogabit invitam.
at tu dolebis, cum rogaberis nulla.
scelesta, vae te, quae tibi manet vita? 15
quis nunc te adibit? cui videberis bella?
quem nunc amabis? cuius esse diceris?
quem basiabis? cui labella mordebis?
at tu, Catulle, destinatus obdura.

10

Varus me meus ad suos amores
visum duxerat e foro otiosum,
scortillum, ut mihi tum repente visum est,
non sane illepidum neque invenustum,
huc ut venimus, incidere nobis 5
sermones varii, in quibus, quid esset
iam Bithynia, quo modo se haberet,
et quonam mihi profuisset aere.
respondi id quod erat, nihil neque ipsis
nec praetoribus esse nec cohorti, 10
cur quisquam caput unctius referret,
praesertim quibus esset irrumator
praetor, nec faceret pili cohortem.
'at certe tamen,' inquiunt 'quod illic
natum dicitur esse, comparasti 15
ad lecticam homines.' ego, ut puellae
unum me facerem beatiorem,
'non' inquam 'mihi tam fuit maligne
ut, provincia quod mala incidisset,
non possem octo homines parare rectos.' 20
at mi nullus erat nec hic neque illic
fractum qui veteris pedem grabati
in collo sibi collocare posset.

AS

hic illa, ut decuit cinaediorem,
'quaeso' inquit mihi, 'mi Catulle, paulum 25
istos commoda: nam volo ad Serapim
deferri.' 'mane' inquii puellae,
'istud quod modo dixeram me habere,
fugit me ratio: meus sodalis –
Cinna est Gaius – is sibi paravit. 30
verum, utrum illius an mei, quid ad me?
utor tam bene quam mihi pararim.
sed tu insulsa male et molesta vivis,
per quam non licet esse neglegentem.'

11

Furi et Aureli, comites Catulli,
sive in extremos penetrabit Indos,
litus ut longe resonante Eoa
tunditur unda,
sive in Hyrcanos Arabesve molles, 5
seu Sagas sagittiferosve Parthos,
sive quae septemgeminus colorat
aequora Nilus,
sive trans altas gradietur Alpes,
Caesaris visens monimenta magni, 10
Gallicum Rhenum horribile aequor ultimosque Britannos,
omnia haec, quaecumque feret voluntas
caelitum, temptare simul parati,
pauca nuntiate meae puellae 15
non bona dicta.
cum suis vivat valeatque moechis,
quos simul complexa tenet trecentos,
nullum amans vere, sed identidem omnium
ilia rumpens; 20

AS

nec meum respectet, ut ante, amorem,
qui illius culpa cecidit velut prati
ultimi flos, praetereunte postquam
tactus aratro est.

17

O Colonia, quae cupis ponte ludere longo,
et salire paratum habes, sed vereris inepta
crura ponticuli axulis stantis in redivivis,
ne supinus eat cavaque in palude recumbat:
sic tibi bonus ex tua pons libidine fiat,   5
in quo vel Salisubsali sacra suscipiantur,
munus hoc mihi maximi da, Colonia, risus.
quendam municipem meum de tuo volo ponte
ire praecipitem in lutum per caputque pedesque,
verum totius ut lacus putidaeque paludis   10
lividissima maximeque est profunda vorago.
insulsissimus est homo, nec sapit pueri instar
bimuli tremula patris dormientis in ulna.
cui cum sit viridissimo nupta flore puella
et puella tenellulo delicatior haedo,   15
adservanda nigerrimis diligentius uvis,
ludere hanc sinit ut lubet, nec pili facit uni,
nec se sublevat ex sua parte, sed velut alnus
in fossa Liguri iacet suppernata securi,
tantundem omnia sentiens quam si nulla sit usquam;   20
talis iste meus stupor nil videt, nihil audit,
ipse qui sit, utrum sit an non sit, id quoque nescit.
nunc eum volo de tuo ponte mittere pronum,
si pote stolidum repente excitare veternum,
et supinum animum in gravi derelinquere caeno,   25
ferream ut soleam tenaci in voragine mula.

34

Dianae sumus in fide
puellae et pueri integri:
Dianam pueri integri
puellaeque canamus.

o Latonia, maximi   5
magna progenies Iovis,
quam mater prope Deliam
deposivit olivam,

montium domina ut fores
silvarumque virentium   10
saltuumque reconditorum
amniumque sonantum:

tu Lucina dolentibus
Iuno dicta puerperis,
tu potens Trivia et notho es   15
dicta lumine Luna.

tu cursu, dea, menstruo
metiens iter annuum,
rustica agricolae bonis
tecta frugibus exples.   20

sis quocumque tibi placet
sancta nomine, Romulique,
antique ut solita es, bona
sospites ope gentem.

A
Level

40

quaenam te mala mens, miselle Ravide,
agit praecipitem in meos iambos?
quis deus tibi non bene advocatus
vecordem parat excitare rixam?
an ut pervenias in ora vulgi? 5
quid vis? qualubet esse notus optas?
eris, quandoquidem meos amores
cum longa voluisti amare poena.

62

Vesper adest, iuvenes, consurgite: Vesper Olympo
exspectata diu vix tandem lumina tollit.
surgere iam tempus, iam pingues linquere mensas,
iam veniet virgo, iam dicetur hymenaeus.
Hymen o Hymenaee, Hymen ades o Hymenaee! 5

cernitis, innuptae, iuvenes? consurgite contra;
nimirum Oetaeos ostendit Noctifer ignes.
sic certe est; viden ut perniciter exsiluere?
non temere exsiluere, canent quod vincere par est.
Hymen o Hymenaee, Hymen ades o Hymenaee! 10

non facilis nobis, aequales, palma parata est:
aspicite, innuptae secum ut meditata requirunt.
non frustra meditantur: habent memorabile quod sit;
nec mirum, penitus quae tota mente laborant.
nos alio mentes, alio divisimus aures; 15
iure igitur vincemur: amat victoria curam.
quare nunc animos saltem convertite vestros;
dicere iam incipient, iam respondere decebit.
Hymen o Hymenaee, Hymen ades o Hymenaee!

Hespere, quis caelo fertur crudelior ignis? 20
qui natam possis complexu avellere matris,
complexu matris retinentem avellere natam,
et iuveni ardenti castam donare puellam.
quid faciunt hostes capta crudelius urbe?
Hymen o Hymenaee, Hymen ades o Hymenaee! 25

Hespere, quis caelo lucet iucundior ignis?
qui desponsa tua firmes conubia flamma,
quae pepigere viri, pepigerunt ante parentes,

**A
Level**

nec iunxere prius quam se tuus extulit ardor.
quid datur a divis felici optatius hora?   30
Hymen o Hymenaee, Hymen ades o Hymenaee!

Hesperus e nobis, aequales, abstulit unam.
* * * * * * * *

* * * * * * * *

namque tuo adventu vigilat custodia semper,
nocte latent fures, quos idem saepe revertens,
Hespere, mutato comprendis nomine Eous   35
at lubet innuptis ficto te carpere questu.
quid tum, si carpunt, tacita quem mente requirunt?
Hymen o Hymenaee, Hymen ades o Hymenaee!

ut flos in saeptis secretus nascitur hortis,
ignotus pecori, nullo convulsus aratro,   40
quem mulcent aurae, firmat sol, educat imber;
multi illum pueri, multae optavere puellae:
idem cum tenui carptus defloruit ungui,
nulli illum pueri, nullae optavere puellae:
sic virgo, dum intacta manet, dum cara suis est;   45
cum castum amisit polluto corpore florem,
nec pueris iucunda manet, nec cara puellis.
Hymen o Hymenaee, Hymen ades o Hymenaee!

ut vidua in nudo vitis quae nascitur arvo,
numquam se extollit, numquam mitem educat uvam,   50
sed tenerum prono deflectens pondere corpus
iam iam contingit summum radice flagellum;
hanc nulli agricolae, nulli coluere iuvenci:
at si forte eadem est ulmo coniuncta marito,
multi illam agricolae, multi coluere iuvenci: 55
sic virgo dum intacta manet, dum inculta senescit;
cum par conubium maturo tempore adepta est,

cara viro magis et minus est invisa parenti.
et tu ne pugna cum tali coniuge, virgo.
non aequum est pugnare, pater cui tradidit ipse,   60
ipse pater cum matre, quibus parere necesse est.
virginitas non tota tua est, ex parte parentum est,
tertia pars patris est, pars est data tertia matri,
tertia sola tua est: noli pugnare duobus,
qui genero sua iura simul cum dote dederunt.   65
Hymen o Hymenaee, Hymen ades o Hymenaee!

64

saepe illam perhibent ardenti corde furentem
clarisonas imo fudisse e pectore voces,   125
ac tum praeruptos tristem conscendere montes,
unde aciem in pelagi vastos protenderet aestus,
tum tremuli salis adversas procurrere in undas
mollia nudatae tollentem tegmina surae,
atque haec extremis maestam dixisse querellis,   130
frigidulos udo singultus ore cientem:
'sicine me patriis avectam, perfide, ab aris
perfide, deserto liquisti in litore, Theseu?
sicine discedens neglecto numine divum,
immemor a! devota domum periuria portas?   135
nullane res potuit crudelis flectere mentis
consilium? tibi nulla fuit clementia praesto,
immite ut nostri vellet miserescere pectus?
at non haec quondam blanda promissa dedisti
voce mihi, non haec miserae sperare iubebas,   140
sed conubia laeta, sed optatos hymenaeos,
quae cuncta aerii discerpunt irrita venti.
nunc iam nulla viro iuranti femina credat,
nulla viri speret sermones esse fideles;

**A
Level**

quis dum aliquid cupiens animus praegestit apisci,   145
nil metuunt iurare, nihil promittere parcunt:
sed simul ac cupidae mentis satiata libido est,
dicta nihil metuere, nihil periuria curant.
certe ego te in medio versantem turbine leti
eripui, et potius germanum amittere crevi,   150
quam tibi fallaci supremo in tempore dessem.
pro quo dilaceranda feris dabor alitibusque
praeda, neque iniacta tumulabor mortua terra.
quaenam te genuit sola sub rupe leaena,
quod mare conceptum spumantibus exspuit undis,   155
quae Syrtis, quae Scylla rapax, quae vasta Charybdis,
talia qui reddis pro dulci praemia vita?
si tibi non cordi fuerant conubia nostra,
saeva quod horrebas prisci praecepta parentis,
at tamen in vestras potuisti ducere sedes,   160
quae tibi iucundo famularer serva labore,
candida permulcens liquidis vestigia lymphis,
purpureave tuum consternens veste cubile.
sed quid ego ignaris nequiquam conquerar auris,
externata malo, quae nullis sensibus auctae   165
nec missas audire queunt nec reddere voces?
ille autem prope iam mediis versatur in undis,
nec quisquam apparet vacua mortalis in alga.
sic nimis insultans extremo tempore saeva
fors etiam nostris invidit questibus aures.   170
Iuppiter omnipotens, utinam ne tempore primo
Gnosia Cecropiae tetigissent litora puppes,
indomito nec dira ferens stipendia tauro
perfidus in Cretam religasset navita funem,
nec malus hic celans dulci crudelia forma   175
consilia in nostris requiesset sedibus hospes!
nam quo me referam? quali spe perdita nitor?
Idaeosne petam montes? at gurgite lato

discernens ponti truculentum dividit aequor.
an patris auxilium sperem? quemne ipsa reliqui   180
respersum iuvenem fraterna caede secuta?
coniugis an fido consoler memet amore?
quine fugit lentos incurvans gurgite remos?
praeterea nullo colitur sola insula tecto,
nec patet egressus pelagi cingentibus undis.   185
nulla fugae ratio, nulla spes: omnia muta,
omnia sunt deserta, ostentant omnia letum.
non tamen ante mihi languescent lumina morte,
nec prius a fesso secedent corpore sensus,
quam iustam a divis exposcam prodita multam   190
caelestumque fidem postrema comprecer hora.
quare facta virum multantes vindice poena
Eumenides, quibus anguino redimita capillo
frons exspirantes praeportat pectoris iras,
huc huc adventate, meas audite querellas,   195
quas ego, vae misera, extremis proferre medullis
cogor inops, ardens, amenti caeca furore.
quae quoniam verae nascuntur pectore ab imo,
vos nolite pati nostrum vanescere luctum,
sed quali solam Theseus me mente reliquit,   200
tali mente, deae, funestet seque suosque.'
has postquam maesto profudit pectore voces,
supplicium saevis exposcens anxia factis,
annuit invicto caelestum numine rector;
quo motu tellus atque horrida contremuerunt   205
aequora concussitque micantia sidera mundus.
ipse autem caeca mentem caligine Theseus
consitus oblito dimisit pectore cuncta,
quae mandata prius constanti mente tenebat,
dulcia nec maesto sustollens signa parenti   210
sospitem Erechtheum se ostendit visere portum.
namque ferunt olim, classi cum moenia divae

linquentem natum ventis concrederet Aegeus,
talia complexum iuveni mandata dedisse:
'nate mihi longa iucundior unice vita,   215
nate, ego quem in dubios cogor dimittere casus,
reddite in extrema nuper mihi fine senectae,
quandoquidem fortuna mea ac tua fervida virtus
eripit invito mihi te, cui languida nondum
lumina sunt nati cara saturata figura,   220
non ego te gaudens laetanti pectore mittam,
nec te ferre sinam fortunae signa secundae,
sed primum multas expromam mente querellas,
canitiem terra atque infuso pulvere foedans,
inde infecta vago suspendam lintea malo,   225
nostros ut luctus nostraeque incendia mentis
carbasus obscurata dicet ferrugine Hibera.
quod tibi si sancti concesserit incola Itoni,
quae nostrum genus ac sedes defendere Erecthei
annuit, ut tauri respergas sanguine dextram,   230
tum vero facito ut memori tibi condita corde
haec vigeant mandata, nec ulla oblitteret aetas;
ut simul ac nostros invisent lumina colles,
funestam antennae deponant undique vestem,
candidaque intorti sustollant vela rudentes,   235
quam primum cernens ut laeta gaudia mente
agnoscam, cum te reducem aetas prospera sistet.'
haec mandata prius constanti mente tenentem
Thesea ceu pulsae ventorum flamine nubes
aereum nivei montis liquere cacumen.   240
at pater, ut summa prospectum ex arce petebat,
anxia in assiduos absumens lumina fletus,
cum primum infecti conspexit lintea veli,
praecipitem sese scopulorum e vertice iecit,
amissum credens immiti Thesea fato.   245
sic funesta domus ingressus tecta paterna

morte ferox Theseus, qualem Minoidi luctum
obtulerat mente immemori, talem ipse recepit.
quae tum prospectans cedentem maesta carinam
multiplices animo volvebat saucia curas. 250
at parte ex alia florens volitabat Iacchus
cum thiaso Satyrorum et Nysigenis Silenis,
te quaerens, Ariadna, tuoque incensus amore.
Thyades huic passim lymphata mente furebant
euhoe bacchantes, euhoe capita inflectentes. 255
harum pars tecta quatiebant cuspide thyrsos,
pars e divulso iactabant membra iuvenco,
pars sese tortis serpentibus incingebant,
pars obscura cavis celebrabant orgia cistis,
orgia quae frustra cupiunt audire profani; 260
plangebant aliae proceris tympana palmis,
aut tereti tenues tinnitus aere ciebant;
multis raucisonos efflabant cornua bombos
barbaraque horribili stridebat tibia cantu.

A Level

70

nulli se dicit mulier mea nubere malle
    quam mihi, non si se Iuppiter ipse petat.
dicit: sed mulier cupido quod dicit amanti,
    in vento et rapida scribere oportet aqua.

76

siqua recordanti benefacta priora voluptas
    est homini, cum se cogitat esse pium,
nec sanctam violasse fidem, nec foedere nullo
    divum ad fallendos numine abusum homines,
multa parata manent in longa aetate, Catulle,   5
    ex hoc ingrato gaudia amore tibi.
nam quaecumque homines bene cuiquam aut dicere possunt
    aut facere, haec a te dictaque factaque sunt.
omnia quae ingratae perierunt credita menti.
    quare iam te cur amplius excrucies?   10
quin tu animo offirmas atque istinc te ipse reducis,
    et dis invitis desinis esse miser?
difficile est longum subito deponere amorem,
    difficile est, verum hoc qua lubet efficias:
una salus haec est. hoc est tibi pervincendum,   15
    hoc facias, sive id non pote sive pote.
o di, si vestrum est misereri, aut si quibus umquam
    extremam iam ipsa in morte tulistis opem,
me miserum aspicite et, si vitam puriter egi,
    eripite hanc pestem perniciemque mihi,   20
quae mihi subrepens imos ut torpor in artus
    expulit ex omni pectore laetitias.
non iam illud quaero, contra me ut diligat illa,
    aut, quod non potis est, esse pudica velit:

ipse valere opto et taetrum hunc deponere morbum.   25
   o di, reddite mi hoc pro pietate mea.

85

odi et amo. quare id faciam, fortasse requiris.
   nescio, sed fieri sentio et excrucior.

88

quid facit is, Gelli, qui cum matre atque sorore
   prurit, et abiectis pervigilat tunicis?
quid facit is, patruum qui non sinit esse maritum?
   ecquid scis quantum suscipiat sceleris?
suscipit, o Gelli, quantum non ultima Tethys   5
   nec genitor Nympharum abluit Oceanus:
nam nihil est quicquam sceleris quo prodeat ultra,
   non si demisso se ipse voret capite.

89

Gellius est tenuis: quid ni? cui tam bona mater
   tamque valens vivat tamque venusta soror
tamque bonus patruus tamque omnia plena puellis
   cognatis, quare is desinat esse macer?
qui ut nihil attingat, nisi quod fas tangere non est,   5
   quantumvis quare sit macer invenies.

91

non ideo, Gelli, sperabam te mihi fidum
   in misero hoc nostro, hoc perdito amore fore,

quod te cognossem bene constantemve putarem
   aut posse a turpi mentem inhibere probro;
sed neque quod matrem nec germanam esse videbam   5
   hanc tibi, cuius me magnus edebat amor.
et quamvis tecum multo coniungerer usu,
   non satis id causae credideram esse tibi.
tu satis id duxti: tantum tibi gaudium in omni
   culpa est, in quacumque est aliquid sceleris.   10

107

si quicquam cupido optantique optigit umquam
   insperanti, hoc est gratum animo proprie.
quare hoc est gratum nobisque est carius auro
   quod te restituis, Lesbia, mi cupido.
restituis cupido atque insperanti, ipsa refers te   5
   nobis. o lucem candidiore nota!
quis me uno vivit felicior aut magis hac res
   optandas vita dicere quis poterit?

Commentary Notes

Poem 1

The opening poem dedicates the book to the Roman polymath, poet and prose author Cornelius Nepos (110–24 BC). The poem is a typical 'dedicatory' piece, similar in tone and content to the opening poem in Meleager's 'Garland' (*Greek Anthology* 4.1). A small portion survives of Nepos' *de viris illustribus*, originally in sixteen books, and Nepos even mentions Catullus at one point (*Atticus* 12.4). The text referred to in this poem is probably the *Chronica*, which apparently dated events in the ancient Greek and Roman worlds – **omne aevum** – and qualifies as **laboriosis**. Roman poets tended to dedicate their work to a named patron: Lucretius' dedicatee was Memmius (who makes unflattering appearances in Catullus (10, 28)), Maecenas was patron to Horace and Virgil, while Tibullus wrote for M. Valerius Messala Corvinus. For more on Nepos and Catullus, see Wiseman, *Catullus and His World* (1979: 154–66).

This poem is informal in tone: the question-and-answer, the colloquial use of **esse aliquid** and the sudden exclamation **Iuppiter!**, the diminutive *libellus* and the self-disparaging tone of **meas nugas** and **quidquid hoc libelli**. The word **libelli** at the end of line 8 recalls **libellum** at the end of line 1 and seems to mark the end of the poem – only for the poet to add two further lines which undercut the modesty and casualness of lines 1–8 with a prayer for immortality (or at least a longer poetic life). The poem discusses both the physical book and also the poetry it contains with clever ambiguity: the book itself is 'polished' **(arida modo pumice expolitum)** and the poetry is metaphorically 'polished': the book is **lepidum** and **novum**, as is the poetry. The physical book will be lucky to last more than a generation, but the poetry may well last forever. The poem also plays with the language of the influential Greek poet Callimachus: the Latin word **lepidum** reminds us of the similar Greek word *leptaleēn* used of the Muse by Callimachus *Aetia* fr. 1.23.

Metre: hendecasyllables

1   cui dono is a question for the poet to answer in line 3. The verb is in the indicative – 'to whom am I dedicating ...?' – and so is confirming a decision already made thanks to the past kindness of Nepos (3–4), although the present indicative can also indicate future intention ('to whom should I dedicate ...?'). **lepidum** indicates 'elegant' both of the volume and of its contents, while **novum** may be an allusion to the *novi poetae* of whom Catullus was a leader. The diminutive *-llum* suffix on **libellum** shows a typical taste for small-scale poetry rather than the bombast of an Antimachus (poem 95b.2) or a Volusius (poems 36, 95.7–8).

2   The stone may be 'dry' but the poetry is not and the book is **expolitum** both literally ('polished using dry pumice-stone') and also 'polished' in its literary style. Poem 22 criticises the poet Suffenus for producing books which are polished on the outside but full of crass rubbish inside: Catullus sees his poetry as excellent in both respects.

3   Corneli (the vocative case of Cornelius) addresses Cornelius Nepos (see above for details). The direct address is further stressed with the use of **tibi ... tu ...**

4   Ironic modesty, as in line 8; the poems were mere **nugas** but Nepos thought they 'were something' (i.e. had some value). The point here is the contrast with the *magnum opus* of Nepos (5–7) in a spirit of deference from poet to patron.

5   iam tum cum means 'even then, when' and adds a ponderous heavy rhythm to the line. The work of Nepos is said to be something which took courage (**ausus es**) and which nobody else tackled (**unus Italorum**).

6 **explicare** continues the series of 'book' metaphors as it means 'to unroll a scroll' (*OLD* s.v. 'explico' 1b) as well as 'to set out' (*OLD* s.v. 8). **omne aevum** seems to mean 'the whole of history' and the achievement here is the compression involved in covering everything in three books.

7 'Scholarly, by Jove, and hard work.' **laboriosis** may mean both 'hard to write' and also 'hard to read': for modern assessment of his writing see *OCD* s.v. 'Cornelius Nepos'.

8 More poetic modesty: **libelli** is a partitive genitive with **quidquid** ('whatever (sort) of a book', i.e. 'this book, such as it is'), while **qualecumque** casts doubt on the quality ('of whatever quality it is').

9 **patrona virgo** is usually read as referring to one of the Muses, the nine female deities who were the sources of artistic inspiration: Lucretius similarly addresses the Muse Calliope (6.92–5). The term **patrona** suggests that the Muse fulfils the function of a Roman *patronus* towards the poet who is her *cliens*: these terms refer to a political and social relationship of mutual benefit between men of different orders (see *OCD* s.v. 'patronus' and 'cliens') and the poet's use of the term is the first of many such appropriations of political and financial terms in his poetry. The text is, however, highly suspect: Trappes-Lomax plausibly suggests that the original reading may perhaps have been *o Thaleia virgo* as Thaleia was the Muse of light verse and comedy.

10 **maneat** is subjunctive expressing a wish ('may it last'). **plus uno ... saeclo** is another modest expression of ambition: not 'forever' but simply 'more than one generation'. This diffidence contrasts strongly with the confident assertion of Horace (*Odes* 3.30) that his poetry will last as long as Rome itself.

A
Level

Poem 5

The first poem in the collection to name (**Lesbia**) Catullus' girlfriend. The poem is a tiny masterpiece of (attempted) persuasion – the argument being that life is too short to waste on anything less important than love, and that the poet and his girl represent the young rebelling against disapproving old men. The use of financial language – from the abacus-style counting of the kisses to the terms **aestimemus** and **conturbabimus** – also marks a deliberate attempt to hijack serious language for use in areas which many Romans would consider unserious. He speaks about the 'excessively strict old men' in terms which they understand and in a provocative way. The poem is recalled and 'answered' in poem 7, where the same themes are once again discussed.

Metre: hendecasyllables

1 The verbs are jussive subjunctives, framing the line with parallel wishes for life and love, and setting up the 'we' which is the poet and his beloved against the unnamed older folk.

2 The three-word line and the hissing sibilants well suggest the rambling disapproval (**rumores**) of the old men. **severiorum** is comparative of *severus* and suggests 'more strict (than anyone should be)' or 'too strict'.

3 **unius assis** is a genitive of value, with a neat juxtaposition of **omnes unius** to show that *all* the **rumores** are only worth a *single as* (the smallest Roman coin). **aestimemus** is another jussive subjunctive. The poet here, as at lines 7–11, uses the language of accounting.

4–5 **occidere** is from *cadere* and so means 'set' or 'die'. The line is perfectly phrased: there is only one sun but the repeated appearances make the plural appropriate, while the to and fro of 'falling and returning' is enhanced by the juxtaposition of **occidere et redire**. **possunt** is important: suns are able to do something which we (**nobis**) cannot, and the repeated rebirth of the sun is tartly refused to us, who can die only once (**semel** 5).

5-6 **nobis** is both a possessive dative with **lux** ('our light') and also a dative of agent going with the gerundive **dormienda** (6): 'one perpetual night is to be slept by us'. The final three words of line 5 diminish in length as the light fades and the drastic switch from life to death is evoked in the simple change of **lux/nox** over the line break. The elision of **perpetua una** and the series of long words evoke the stillness of everlasting night.

7-10 The poet asks for kisses in ever increasing quantity, as if the numbers are being calculated before the accounts are destroyed in line 11. The inventory of kisses takes four lines, with extensive repetition of words, to suggest the extensive time to be taken over the repeated kisses themselves, and the adverb **usque** tells us that the kisses are to proceed without any break. The word *basium* denotes an erotic kiss rather than the more chaste *osculum*.

10 **fecerimus** is future perfect indicative and the verb here means 'to make up a total amount' or 'reach a target' (*OLD* s.v. 'facio' 9b).

11 The line is framed by the verbs. The poet will go on to describe the risk of somebody **malus** knowing, but in this line he avows that he and Lesbia are themselves not to know the exact total. *conturbare* means 'to mess up <the accounts>' but it also (*OLD* s.v. 3) means 'to go bankrupt' and nicely suggests the poet breaking the bank of kisses. It may even be echoing the sort of language which the *senes severiores* might use of the lovers. Knowledge is power and the evil ones can work their magic (**invidere**) if they have the facts.

12 **ne quis malus** ('so that no evil man') introduces a purpose clause with subjunctive (**possit**). **invidere** is to 'look in a hostile manner' or even 'cast the evil eye' suggestive of the powerful envy of these prurient old men.

13 **basiorum** is a partitive genitive after **tantum** ('so great an amount of kisses'). **cum ... sciat** is 'in so far as he knows', followed by the accusative **tantum** and infinitive **esse** ('that there are so many'). The verb recalls **ne sciamus** (11).

AS

Poem 6

This poem contrasts well with the erotic poems surrounding it. It purports to be a piece of male banter, seeking to tease one of his friends about his shameful sex life, but the language could be read as also reflecting the views which Flavius might well have of the poet's own sex life as shown in poems 5 and 7. For this sort of jocular banter in poetry, cf. 10, 17, 40, 88, 89, 91.

This poem falls into a pleasing A–B–A structure, whereby lines 1–5 has the poet asking about Flavius' secret lover, lines 6–14 sets out the damning evidence of Flavius' passion and the final three lines return to the initial request to tell all. Nothing is known of the identity of Flavius.

Metre: hendecasyllables

1–3 The sentence is an unfulfilled conditional (**ni** = *nisi*), stating that Flavius must be ashamed of his girlfriend as otherwise he would not be able to keep quiet about her.

1 The line is framed by the two names (**Flavi . . . Catullo**) surrounding the key words **delicias tuas** ('your darling' – the noun is used of his girlfriend's pet sparrow in poems 2 and 3).

2 *illepidus* is the opposite of *lepidus*: Flavius' girl is said to be lacking charm with a term which is applied to poetry (see line 17 and 1.1) as well as to Varus' girlfriend (10.4). **sint** is present subjunctive but refers (like **velles** and **posses** in line 3) to present time.

3 An elegant and forceful line, with the two subjunctives framing a pair of infinitives: Flavius would *want* to talk and be unable *not* to do so.

4 **nescioquid** (literally, 'I know not what') means 'some sort of' and goes with the partitive genitive **febriculosi/scorti**. **febriculosi** must mean 'prone to fevers' or 'sickly' – something seen as unattractive in a lover (cf. 81.3–4, Lucretius 4.1167, Plato *Republic* 474e).

5 *scortum* is properly a prostitute but is commonly used as a pejorative term ('tart') for a girl and the contrast is here heightened by the juxtaposition with **diligis** ('you actually *love* a tart?'). **pudet** is an impersonal verb ('it shames you') and **fateri** is well chosen ('to admit this').

6–11 These lines all form one long sentence: line 6 is an accusative and infinitive reported statement which Flavius' bed 'shouts out' to be true ('For your bed . . . shouts out that you . . .').

6 **non viduas** is a litotes ('not alone' meaning 'with somebody else' and so presumably engaged in sex).

7 The chorus begins with the bed (**cubile**), whose physical silence is futile (**nequiquam tacitum**) as it shouts (**clamat**) your activities. The bed is incapable of human speech (only creaking: see line 11) but its movements convey the message at full volume with effective alliteration of 'c'.

8 The bed betrays its secrets first by its fragrance: garlands and fragrant Syrian perfumes show that this is a bed used for love-making. **olivo** is a suspect reading because Romans did not import olive oil from Syria but produced their own: the poet is perhaps referring to perfumes made from a mixture of (native) olive oil with imported scents from the East.

9–10 The poet points out that the **pulvinus** (the single bolster-type pillow used on a Roman double bed) is indented on both sides because two people have slept on it. **peraeque** is a stronger form of *aeque* ('evenly') and the demonstrative **et hic et illic** evokes the poet pointing out the evidence to his friend. **attritus** (from *attero*) is emphasised in enjambement and well conveys the 'wearing away' by endless rubbing activity – an image which the following words **tremulique quassa** continue.

10–11 The poet indulges in mock-pompous banter. The bed is shaking (**tremuli**) and the creaking (**argutatio**) sound is eloquent testimony against him – with the word also suggesting the legalistic term *arguo* ('I prove' or 'find guilty'). The final word is brilliant: the bed is so busy that it is 'walking' around the room (like a barrister in a court room) and this is conveyed in a third declension abstract noun of apparent gravity and comic effect (cf. *basiationes* at 7.1, *fututiones* 32.8). **quassa** is the past participle of *quatio* and agrees grammatically with **argutatio**, although, in fact, it is the bed which is shaking and the epithet has been transferred (a device known as hypallage).

12 The manuscript reading (*nam inista praevalet*) is nonsense and many modern editions mark the line as irredeemably corrupt. I have printed what seems the most sensible emendation: Ellis' **nam nil stare valet nihil tacere** ('it has no power to stay still, nor to stay silent'), which matches line 11 nicely (in chiastic order: sound – movement – movement sound). The balanced pair of '*nihil*+verb' phrases is also fully in Catullus' style (cf. 17.21, 42.21, 64.146). **nil** is a contracted form of **nihil**.

13 The poet allows Flavius to ask 'why?' so that he can continue the banter, the comments now becoming even more personal and obscene. **ecfututa** is the perfect passive participle of *ecfutuo* ('to wear out with excessive sex') and agrees with the **latera** (literally, 'flanks', but here as often indicates the site of sexual exhaustion). **tam** must go with **ecfututa** – the hyperbaton is itself perhaps indicative of the panting exhaustion of Flavius. **pandas** is present subjunctive ('you would not show') as the apodosis of the conditional whose protasis ('if . . . not . . .') continues on the next line.

14 **ni** (as at line 2) means *nisi* ('if . . . not'): **ni facias quid** means 'if you were not doing some sort of' with the partitive genitive **ineptiarum** ('silliness': cf. 8.1 on this word).

15 The poet rounds off the poem with a conclusion: **quare** ('and so . . .') and a catch-all phrase to describe the girl herself ('whatever you have – good and bad'), which is interesting as, so far, the poet has assumed she is a total embarrassment. **boni malique** are partitive genitives with **quidquid**.

16 **dic nobis** ('tell us') sounds like impatient curiosity – but the poet is shortly going to offer to immortalise the affair in **lepido versu** and so can offer something in return. For the scansion of **vŏlŏ** cf. 17.8–9n.). **amores** recalls (and is equivalent to) **delicias** in line 1.

17 'to summon somebody to heaven' means 'to make immortal'. **lepido** is well chosen: the girl may be **illepidae** (line 2) but the verses will not be. The unspecified **deliciae** can become **amores** by means of **lepido versu**, thus stating and effecting the poetic immortality offered to the silent Flavius.

Poem 7

This poem continues the theme and the content of poem 5 – as if Lesbia had read poem 5 with its demands for innumerable kisses and asked the poet to set a limit to his desires. The poem is different in tone: whereas poem 5 had an urgency and a directness consistent with the poet seeking his pleasures, this poem takes a more relaxed and learned attitude to the whole business of kiss-counting and conveys less of a sense of boisterous yearning. The playfulness remains in the question posed in 1–2 and answered in 3–12, the mock-serious word **basiationes**, the compound adjective **lasarpiciferis**, the sly reference to the **furtivos hominum amores**, the self-description of the poet (in the third person) as **vesano** and the phrase **basia basiare**. The Greek poet Callimachus is alluded to (see lines 4 and 6), who was a massive influence on Roman poets: see Introduction, 'Catullus and the "New Poets"'.

Metre: hendecasyllables

1 The poet poses a direct question to his beloved (cf. 72.7, 85.1). **basiationes** is an abstract word ('kissification' perhaps) formed from the simple noun *basium* ('kiss'): cf. *osculationis* (48.6) and *fututiones* (32.8).

2 **sint** is subjunctive in an indirect question after **quaeris**. **satis superque** ('enough and more than enough', repeated at line 10) is

AS

colloquial in tone, but the phrase is at once undermined by the series of apparent infinities which follow.

3–6 'As many as the sands on the shore' was already a cliché (cf. Homer *Iliad* 2.800, 9.385). Later writers invented new forms of 'as many as' (e.g. Juvenal 10.219–26) but Catullus here injects new life into the old formula by making the sand that of Cyrene, which was the birthplace of the influential Greek poet Callimachus.

4 Silphium (*lasarpicium*) was imported from Cyrene for medical use – the famously bald Julius Caesar, for example, acquired a lot of it thinking (wrongly) that it promoted hair growth. The compound adjective **lasarpiciferis** only occurs here in Latin and may well be a Catullan coinage. The plant became the principal export (and source of income) of Cyrene.

5 The Egyptian god Ammon was associated with Zeus/Jupiter and his temple at Siwa was renowned in the ancient world not least for the oracle, which allegedly told Alexander the Great that he was the son of Zeus Ammon. Jupiter is 'sweltering' (**aestuosi**) because the Sahara Desert is so hot.

6 Battus was the founder of the Greek colony of Cyrene, according to Herodotus (4.150–5) and so his tomb had special veneration there. The reference is also another subtle allusion to the poet Callimachus, who is simply called *Battiades* ('descendant of Battus') at 65.16, 116.2.

7–8 'As many as the stars' is a pleasing simile in itself (found also in Callimachus *Hymn* 4.175–6), but Catullus renders it more relevant and personal to himself with the extra details of the stars looking down on illicit love affairs. The night is conspiratorially silent (**tacet**) and the love affairs are secret ones (**furtivos**) which cannot be practised in the daylight hours when people would see them. This adds weight to the idea that Catullus' Lesbia was the married woman with whom he enjoys a liaison in poem 68 – especially as her love is there (68.145) described as *furtiva munuscula* ('secret little gifts'). She has been identified by many with the notorious Clodia Metelli (see Introduction). Line 7 ends with **nox**, recalling the *lux/nox* dichotomy of 5.5–6.

9–10 **basia basiare** (literally, 'to kiss kisses') is an example of the cognate accusative: the main verb is **satis est**, followed by **te** with the infinitive ('it is enough . . . that you should kiss so many kisses'). The word **basia** picks up **basiationes** from line 1 and the repetition of the word is a nice enactment of the repeated kisses which the poet demands. Catullus here allows that his passionate behaviour is mad (**vesano**) as he does at poem 100.7: the word is also used of ravenous hunger in lions (Virgil *Aeneid* 9.340), and in this studied piece of elegant literature the effect is ironic.

11–12 The ending of the poem recalls poem 5 strongly and seals its status as a continuation of that poem: **curiosi** reminds us of the phrase **senum severiorum** (5.2) and the 'wicked' (**malus**) man prone to envy (**invidere** (5.12)) is here given a 'wicked tongue' (**mala lingua**) to use in his witchcraft (**fascinare**). A *fascinum* was a phallic-shaped charm worn around the neck to ward off evil, serving a function somewhat like the phalluses found on the walls of Pompeii, and the verb **fascinare** means something like 'bewitch' or 'cast a spell on'. The metre shows that the term **mala . . . lingua** is in the nominative case: it becomes a second subject of the verb **possint**.

Poem 8

The rhythm of this poem is 'limping iambics' or scazons: five iambic feet followed by a trochee. The effect of this 'falling' cadence is powerful and suits well the lame lover's lament.

This poem is not simple. It reads as a serious psychological poem, expressing the poet's inner conflict of love and anger: the poet confesses his love (5) and looks back in erotic nostalgia (4–8, 17–18), which ultimately forces him to admit that his attempts to 'harden his heart' against her are unsuccessful as they need to be reaffirmed in the final

AS

line. His love for her has transmuted into anger and hatred as he relishes the sexual Sahara which (he claims) awaits her once she has spurned his affections. This wishful thinking is flawed, at least if the girl addressed is the same successfully promiscuous one whom he addresses elsewhere (see 11.17–20).

Alternatively, the poem can be read more simply as a piece of persuasion seeking to win back his lover's affections with threats to leave her lonely. The poet's language is angry (**scelesta, vae te**) but expresses his sad indignation rather than any lasting venom, and his wrath only serves to prove his enduring love.

The poem is a text of great sophistication. The poet addresses himself in the second person (1–11) and then his girl (12–18) in the second person, referring to himself in the third person (12–13) before talking to himself again in the second person (19). There is neat use of closural devices such as ring composition (3–8), there is good use of indignant rhetorical questions (15–18) to her which allow for the possibility of dialogue, but the harsher imperatives to himself (1–2, 9–11, 19) close down discussion. Where the poet describes himself (12–13) it is in terms suggestive of the image he wishes to project rather than the truth behind it. He is playing a part in a drama which both reveals and conceals his own feelings.

1   The poet addresses himself by name in the vocative case, a device also used in 76.5 and setting up the inner conflict which the poem will explore. **miser** indicates not just 'unhappy' but specifically 'lovesick' (cf. 64.140, Lucretius 4.1076: cf. the 'mad' Catullus of 7.10). **desinas** (and **ducas** in line 2) are both present subjunctives used as an order but less aggressive than an imperative would be. **ineptire** here means 'acting like a fool'.

2   A neatly constructed line, with the verbs sandwiching the central strong juxtaposition of **perisse perditum**: 'what you see to have gone you should regard as gone'. **ducas** here means 'regard' or 'think'.

3   The metaphor of sunlight denotes good fortune (cf. 107.6, 68.148). The plural **soles** indicates repeated instances (as at 5.4) of sunshine, and

candidi ('white' or 'bright') is a word also used of beautiful girls (68.70) and even nights of passion (Propertius 2.15.1); combined with **soles**, it perhaps indicates 'days of gorgeous sunshine'.

4 ventitabas is the 'frequentative' form of *venio*, indicating that the poet constantly followed the girl at her bidding (**quo puella ducebat**).

5 This thought follows on from line 4: the poet willingly went where she led as he loved her more than any woman will ever be loved: the poet looks both backwards with the past participle **amata** and then forwards with the strong future indicative **amabitur**, the repetition of the word enhancing the continuing force of the poet's love. **nobis** is dative of agent: and the plural form of the pronoun simply means 'me', as often in Latin poetry (cf. 107.3, 107.6).

6 iocosa suggests 'fun' or 'amusement' and is a coy word to describe erotic activity (as at Ovid *Ars Amatoria* 2.724: see Adams *The Latin Sexual Vocabulary* 161–3). For similar uses of words denoting 'fooling around' for sexual behaviour, cf. the use of *ludere* at 17.17, 68.17. The quantity of 'fun' is suggested by **multa. fiebant** ('were done') is passive in tone, giving nothing away at this stage about the wishes of the participants, which are revealed in the next line.

7 An example of the double standard: the (male) poet expressed his desire (**volebas**) and the girl 'did not say no'.

8 This line repeats line 3 with the substitution for **quondam** of the stronger word **vere**, which adds powerful assonance (**fulsērĕ vērē**); the effect of the repetition is to mark the end of the first section of the poem. **fulsere** is the short form of the third person plural perfect of *fulgeo* (cf. 10.5).

9 The past tenses of lines 3–8 are now brought sharply up to date with the temporal adverbs **nunc iam** and the present tense **non vult** (picking up **nolebat** from line 7). The stark verb **non vult** ('says no') clearly refers to sex. The poet addresses himself with a string of five imperatives (**noli ... sectare ... vive ... perfer, obdura**), which are more impatient

than the jussive subjunctives of lines 1–2. **impotens** denotes 'powerless'
to do anything about this sudden turn of events except to join the girl
in 'saying no'.

10   **sectare** is the singular imperative of *sector*. The lover-as-hunter
is a common theme in poetry, and can denote the lengths to which
the devoted lover will go to catch his girl (see, e.g., Ovid *Ars Amatoria*
1.43–50, Horace *Satires* 1.2.105–8). There is nothing wrong with chasing
after one who flees, unless (as here) the quarry will never acquiesce in
being caught and when (as here) the hunter is a weakling (**impotens**).
miser here (as at line 1) means 'lovesick': for **vive** meaning 'spend your
life being' cf. 10.33.

11   The poet's desperate need for strength is perhaps echoed with the
repeated *ob-* sounds and with the pairing of the two imperatives **perfer**,
obdura in asyndeton. **obstinata mente** is in the ablative ('with resolute
mind'). **obdura** is formed from *durus* and denotes 'harden your heart'.

12   Catullus moves from addressing himself to addressing the girl
directly with a blunt 'goodbye, girl', followed by a statement describing
Catullus in the third person; he moves from telling himself to **obdura**
to telling his girl that he now **obdurat**.

13   The verbs here are confident future indicatives predicting the girl's
coming misery. **requiret** suggests 'come looking for you', while **rogabit**
has the sense of seeking her company. **invitam** picks up **non volt** from
line 9.

14   **rogaberis** is the second singular future passive of *rogo*: 'you will be
asked', while **nulla** (agreeing with the feminine subject of the verb) is
colloquial here for 'not at all' as at 17.20.

15   The poet's feelings begin to show through here: **scelesta** here
means 'wretched one' and **vae te** means little more than 'woe is you' (**vae**
and 'woe' are connected etymologically). **manet** means 'is waiting for
you in the future' (cf. 76.5). The poet's feelings are not simply condolence,
however, as line 5 and lines 16–18 show.

16–18 The poet fantasises with a rising sequence of amatory progression, couched in an indignant series of short questions, with barking repetition of interrogative words (**quis … cui … quem … cuius … quem … cui**), mocking her future while also imagining what she will *not* be doing with him. He begins with the admiring approach (16), then the forming of a bond (17) and finally the sexual encounter (18).

16   cui videberis bella means 'to whom will you look pretty?' **bella** is a more colloquial word for 'pretty' (cf. 43.2, 78.3) than the more formal *pulcher.*

17   There is a threat in this line: this girl was loved by the poet (line 5) but she now faces a future with nobody to love her.

18   The poet's imagination now sees her in bed with another man: for **basiabis**, cf. **basia** in poem 5 and **basiationes** in 7. **labella mordebis** takes the kissing a stage further with lip-biting and it is clear by now that the poet is recalling her past sexual habits as well as predicting her bleak future. For lip-biting, cf. 68.127, Lucretius 4.1109; Plutarch tells us in his *Life of Pompey* (2.2) that Pompey's mistress Flora never left his embrace without bearing the marks of his teeth.

19   The poet closes the poem by once again addressing himself and echoes his earlier words (**at tu** (cf. 14), **Catulle** (cf. 1), **destinatus obdura** (recalling **obstinata … obdura** (11)) and returns the poet to his (futile) wish to harden his heart.

Poem 10

Unlike Flavius in poem 6, Varus is happy to show off his new girlfriend, and the poet tries unsuccessfully to impress her. The poem is a pleasant self-mocking sketch of Catullus and his friends, fully in the self-deprecating, humorous style of satire (cf. Horace *Satires* 1.9 for a comparable street scene). The poet's feelings towards the girl change

AS

from approval (4) to disapproval (**cinaediorem** 24), to insults (33) as she corners him into embarrassment. This sequence of feelings and the use of direct speech make this a lively and dramatic poem, and the mockery is directed at the poet himself rather than at the girl who catches him out in his lies. For other poems expressing this kind of self-mockery, cf. 8, 44, 50, 51.

1–2 **Varus** also appears in poem 22 and may be the Alfenus Varus addressed in poem 30 or else the Varus who was a friend of Virgil and Horace; his only function in this poem is to have a new girlfriend who attracts the poet's attention. Understand the Latin thus: 'my Varus had taken me from the forum, where I was at a loose end (**otiosum** agreeing with **me**), to his girlfriend (**ad suos amores**) to see her' (**visum** is the supine of *video* used here to indicate purpose).

3 **scortillum** (which occurs only here in Latin) alludes to **suos amores** and is the diminutive of *scortum* (a prostitute) – with the diminutive form toning down the abusive quality of the word. **scortillum** suggests that the girl is attractive and also available: the rest of the line shows that this was Catullus' first sight of her, **repente** meaning here 'at once'.

4 Any pejorative edge in **scortillum** is set aside as the poet credits the girl as 'not without charm and elegance'. The poet's attempt to look cool and composed is well conveyed by the litotes **non sane illepidum** to mean *lepidum* and **neque invenustum** to mean *et venustum*. *lepidus* and *venustus* are key words of approval, suggesting grace, wit, charm and urbane elegance – see 1.1, 13.6, 22.2, 31.12, 50.7, 78.1–2, 86.3, 89.2 – just as their opposites are terms of derision (e.g. 6.2, 12.5, 36.17) linked at times to the rustic boor (e.g. 22.14). **non sane** has the sense 'certainly not . . .'.

5 **ut** here means simply 'when' and **incidēre** is the shorter form of the third person plural perfect (for **incidērunt**).

5–8 A series of indirect questions (**quid . . . quomodo . . . quonam . . .**) indicates the free-flowing conversation. The construction is: 'all sorts of (**varii**) conversations (**sermones**) came to us (**nobis incidere**) including (**in quibus**) . . .'

6–7 quid esset iam Bithynia means 'what was Bithynia like these days' in a very general sense, while **quomodo se haberet** is more focused on 'how it was doing' (see *OLD* s.v. 'habeo' 21b).

8 quonam profuisset aere is very specific ('especially, what financial profit I had made from it') and is the turning point of the conversation. Bithynia was the province (on the Black Sea coast of northern Turkey) where Catullus had been on the staff of the praetorian governor. It is interesting that provincial service was expected to carry substantial financial reward for the Romans.

9 id quod erat ('that which was') simply means 'the truth' and shows the poet starting to turn the conversation towards the character of the governor Memmius. The poet's language is self-excusing ('I told her straight . . .').

9–10 'I replied … that there was nothing (**nihil esse** in indirect statement after **respondi**) for the natives (**ipsis** is possessive dative), nor the praetors, nor the staff (**cohorti**), and no reason why (**cur**) they should bring their head back better oiled (i.e. come home richer)'. The order is significant: if the natives had nothing, then the governing *praetor* got little, and so there would be even less for his staff. The plural **praetoribus** does not mean that there was more than one governor at one time but simply that each successive governor tried to fleece them.

11 For the Roman taste for expensive perfumes and hair oil, cf. 13.11–14 and cf. *uncta patrimonia* at 29.22.

12 irrumator literally means a man who forces another to give him oral sex, and was in common colloquial use for an exploitative superior: cf. 16.1, 28.9–10. The praetor in question was C. Memmius, the patron of the poet Lucretius and a man of literary as well as political ambitions. It is perfectly possible that Memmius was protecting the poor Bithynians from his rapacious staff rather than keeping the profits for himself.

13   *pili facere* is 'to value (see *OLD* s.v. '*facio*' 18c) as being worth a hair' (**pili** is the genitive of value from *pilus -i*) and so means 'to care a jot for'.

14   The riposte to the poet's claim is made by both Varus and the girl as the plural verb **inquiunt** shows.

14–15   'something which is said to have originated in that place': the whole phrase refers to the practice of using litter-bearers. **comparasti** is the shortened form of *comparavisti*.

16   The *lectica* was a sedan-chair or 'litter' carried by several men, thereby allowing the rich to be carried in comfort and be kept safely away from the jostling crowds. Juvenal (1.64–5) has a rich man with six litter-bearers, while Catullus (line 20) foolishly boasts of eight. The litter-chair with eight carriers was (according to Cicero *Verrines* 2.5.27) especially associated with Bithynia.

16–17   The poet freely admits that his aim was to impress Varus' girlfriend. **puellae** is dative – 'so that I could make myself look especially fortunate to the girl'. For *unus* used to strengthen a term, cf. 58.2, Virgil *Aeneid* 1.15–16; **unum** goes here with **me . . . beatiorem**.

18   Having said at lines 9–13 that Bithynia gave no opportunities for money-making, the poet now claims that things were not so bad that he could not get himself some litter-bearers. **non . . . mihi tam fuit maligne ut** means 'things did not go so poorly for me that . . .'. For the colloquial expression of dative + *est* + adverb, cf. 14.10, 23.5, 38.1. *malignus* has the sense of 'stingy' or 'mean' and there is a nice jingle with **mala** in the next line.

19   **incidisset** 'had come my way': for *incidere*, cf. line 5.

20   **rectos** indicates 'standing up straight' (cf. 86.2) and is the bare minimum expected of a litter-bearer.

21–3   After the poet's confident boast comes the truth, spoken only to us, the reading public. He has nobody at all who could carry the 'broken leg of an old bed', let alone eight men to carry a litter.

21   **mi** = *mihi* and is dative of possession with **nullus erat**. **hīc** means 'here' and the phrase means 'neither here (in Rome) nor there (in Bithynia)'.

22   Four words pile on the shame: the bed is only a *grabatus* (a poor man's flimsy camp bed): it is old (**veteris**): his (non-existent) man could not even carry one broken leg, let alone the whole bed, and mention of the 'broken leg' further adds to the air of physical weakness.

23   There is a nice repetition of sounds in **collo . . . collocare**.

24   The girl was described in positive terms in line 4 but is now **cinaediorem**: a pejorative term usually used for sexual reprobates, such as Mamurra and Caesar at 57.1 and here raised to a higher level of indecency with the comparative form. **ut decuit** means here 'as one would expect of . . .' and **hic** has the sense 'at this point'.

25   The girl adopts a tone of easy familiarity with the poet – another sign of her flirty character. **paulum** here means 'for a short time' and **quaeso** ('I ask you') means 'please'. **inquit mihi** most naturally go together ('she said to me').

26   If the text is correct, **commŏdă** is the imperative form: the final syllable is usually long but the shortening here is colloquial (but see also 17.8–9n.).

26–7   Serapis was an Egyptian deity (see *OCD* s.v. 'Sarapis') with a cult following in Italy centred on a temple where cures were sought for illness by sleeping in the temple ('incubation') as in the temple of Asclepius in Greece. Here, the name of the deity stands for the temple dedicated to him. The key verb **deferri** is postponed in enjambement, thus stressing that the **scortillum** wishes 'to be conveyed' there rather than walk – a touch of haughty grandeur which catches the poet by surprise.

28–30   The poet's reply is instantaneous ('wait a moment' **mane**) and he stammers incoherently in the following lines as he tries to frame an acceptable excuse.

28   istud quod modo dixeram me habere means literally: 'as for that which I had just said I have'.

29   fugit me ratio (literally: 'good sense escaped me') simply means, 'I made a mistake'.

30   The poet's nervous language is still plain: he inverts *Gaius Cinna* into **Cinna ... Gaius** and the name **Gaius** has to be scanned in a stammering three-syllable **Gāĭŭs**. Caius Helvius Cinna was a neoteric poet (see poem 95 for praise of his poem *Smyrna*) and by implication a colleague of Catullus in Bithynia. He may also be the same 'Cinna the poet' who was murdered after the assassination of Julius Caesar in 44 BC (as reported by Suetonius *Julius Caesar* 85 and dramatised in Shakespeare *Julius Caesar* Act 3 sc.3).

31   The poet lamely argues that he and Cinna share goods so it does not matter whether (**utrum**) the litter-bearers are 'his' (**illius**) or 'belong to me' (**mei**). **quid ad me?** i.e. *quid ad me (attinet)?* – 'what's it to me?' The excuse falls flat: the poet should be able to supply Cinna's men as if they were his own – but he cannot.

32   tam ... quam is a correlative clause understanding *si* after **quam** with a perfect subjunctive **pararim** (shortened form of *paraverim*) meaning, 'I have use of them just as well as if I had got them for myself.'

33   The poet rounds on the girl, as if the whole conversation were a dirty trick played on him by her, when, in fact, it was all his own fault for bragging. *insulsus* means 'not *salsus*' (cf. 17.12) and so 'lacking in *sal*' (i.e. wit, taste, from the word for salt), amplified by the colloquial adverb **male** here intensifying the pejorative term **insulsa**. For the positive *salsus*, cf. 12.4. **vivis** means 'spend your life being' as at 8.10.

34   For **per** (+ accusative) **licet**, see *OLD* s.v. 'per' 9b: the meaning is 'so far as you are concerned one may not ...'. The poem ends with the key word **neglegentem**: it was all a careless mistake. We know from lines 16–17 that this is not true as he there admitted that he was deliberately showing off to the girl.

AS

Poem 11

Metre: Sapphics: a lyric metre associated with the Greek poet Sappho of Lesbos and also used in the love poem 51 (see note on 22–4 below). It is apt that the same metre is used for one poem (51) expressing passionate love and this poem expressing passionate hatred.

It was something of a commonplace to say that good *amici* would undertake any journey to accompany their friend, even when – especially when – it involved extreme danger and journeys to the ends of the earth: cf. Horace *Odes* 2.6.1–8, *Epodes* 1.11–14, Propertius 1.6.1–4. This poem falls broadly into two sections: the first four stanzas are one giant sentence outlining the friendship and the loyalty of Furius and Aurelius and ending (15–16) with the direct instruction to them, while the final two stanzas convey the harsh words which they are to deliver to his lover: the fourth stanza marks the transition from 'friends' to 'girl'. The request is *a fortiori*: if you could go to the ends of the earth and face extremes of weather, then all the more easily can you deliver a 'few' (**pauca**) words to my girlfriend. The poem sets up a series of contrasts: male friendship versus female love: distant conflicts versus personal strife: the girl's flagrant promiscuity versus the flower of the poet's love.

The poem raises other questions. Why did Catullus involve Furius and Aurelius? Could he not have written a poem directly to his girl? Is he insinuating that Furius and Aurelius were among the '300 lovers' enjoying the girl's favours? What is the point of the travelogue tour of the world in lines 2–12? Is he perhaps suggesting that for him to dismiss his girl (albeit via messengers rather than personally) is a feat which is as hard for him as the extensive adventures outlined here?

Lines 1–14 are striking in their use of epic language: the compound adjectives (**sagittiferos ... septemgeminus**), the epic phrasing (e.g. **voluntas caelitum**), the exotic descriptions of far-flung places, with references to size and distance (**extremos...longe...altas...ultimos**) as well as to national stereotypes (**molles ... sagittiferos**), the use of thundering assonance (**tunditur unda**) and sibilance (6–7), all building up to the 'here and now' grandeur of Roman achievements in the third stanza, with its emphasis on the rebarbartive qualities of what has been faced (**altas ... horribile ... ultimos**). The language of the lines thus produces a poetic recreation of the epic challenges being described: and the lines are, of course, building towards the bathos of 15–20, whose bluntness is all the more shocking for the contrast with what goes before.

The poem can be roughly dated (from the references to Caesar) as being written in the late 50s BC (see notes on lines 10–12).

1 Furius and/or Aurelius appear several times in the poems of Catullus (15, 16, 21, 23, 24, 26) and the poet seems to have a close bantering relationship with these 'companions' (**comites**). Furius is possibly the poet Marcus Furius Bibaculus (see *OCD* s.v. 'Furius Bibaculus, Marcus'): we know nothing of Aurelius.

2 extremos Indos here means 'the furthest Indians'. India was regarded as the Eastern edge of the world (cf. Juvenal 10.1, Horace *Epistles* 1.1.45).

3–4 ut here means 'where' (cf. 17.10). **litus** is the subject of the verb **tunditur**, and **longe resonante Eoa ... unda** all goes together as an instrumental ablative. Translate: 'where the shore is beaten by the far-resounding eastern wave'. The phrase is powerfully written: there is the pounding onomatopoeic repetition of **tunditur unda** and the howling open vowels of **Eoa**.

5 Hyrcans lived on the southern shore of the Caspian Sea. The people of Arabia are termed **molles** ('soft, effeminate'), in line with common stereotyping of Eastern men as perfumed eunuchs (cf. the words used of Aeneas and his Trojans by a suspicious Iarbas in Virgil *Aeneid* 4.215–17 and also by a jealous Turnus at *Aeneid* 12. 97–100).

6 The Sagae were nomadic peoples living in what is now Tashkent on the edge of ancient Persia, while the Parthians lived in what is now north-eastern Iran. The Parthians were notorious for their archery –

most notably the 'Parthian shot', which involved pretending to retreat and then suddenly shooting at the enemy. The Roman general Marcus Crassus lost his life at the battle of Carrhae against the Parthians in 53 BC. The line is notable for the emphatic repetition of **Sagas sag-**.

7–8 Catullus leaves the key name (**Nilus**) to the end of line 8, but the compound adjective **septemgeminus** ('sevenfold') is a strong clue to the identity of the river. **aequora** is artfully ambiguous: if it refers to the 'seas' then it means that the Nile colours the Mediterranean with its silt, and if to the 'plains' of Egypt then it refers to the darkening of the soil when the river floods.

9–12 This stanza has often been taken to allude to Julius Caesar's campaigns (including his bridging of the Rhine in 55 BC (**Rhenum**) and his subsequent invasion of Britain (**Britannos**)) and many editors posit a tentative date for the poem in the late 50s BC. The reference to **Caesaris . . . monimenta** assumes that Julius Caesar has by now been successful in his foreign achievements.

9 altas gradietur Alpes well conveys the imagined 'marching' steps over the 'high Alps', a feat managed by Hannibal in 218 BC.

10 The line is framed by 'great Caesar' and the adjective is possibly ironic: it was a title borne by Alexander and (in Catullus' own day) by Pompey. Only those who consider themselves 'great men' have reasons to have **monimenta** erected, and **visens** suggests a pilgrimage of admiration. For a much less admiring attitude to Caesar, cf. poems 57 and 93.

11–12 The river Rhine was 'Gallic' since it marked the frontier of the province of Gaul: crossing it amounted to an invasion of Germany. Caesar was given Gaul as his province after his consulship in 59 BC and held it for ten years before returning to Rome with his army to begin a civil war in 49 BC. The rhythm is far from elegant: the final -*um* of **Rhenum** elides with the opening syllable of **horribile**, and the -*e* of that word elides into **aequor**. The word **ultimosque** is split over the two lines in what seems an awkward placing of words indicative of a difficult campaign. The 'dreadful sea' in question is the English Channel. Britain was often seen as the furthest point West for the Romans (cf. 29.4, Horace *Odes* 1.35.29–30: for the same combination of rough sea and remote Britons, cf. Horace *Odes* 4.14.47–9 ('the ocean full of sea-monsters roars against the furthest Britons')). The British were also regarded as fearsomely savage in their human sacrifice (Tacitus *Annals* 14.30) and cruelty to strangers (Horace *Odes* 3.4.33).

13–14 omnia haec summarises the suggested challenges of lines 1–12. The potential dangers are then broadened even further with the **quaecumque** clause ('whatever the will of the gods will bring'). **caelitum** ('heaven-dwellers' from *caeles*) is an archaic word for 'gods' and both the unusual choice of word and its enjambement add emphasis.

14 parati is nominative plural agreeing with Furius and Aurelius, who are the subject of the imperative **nuntiate** in the next line. **simul** here amounts to 'alongside (me)', as at 21.5, 46.10, 50.13, 63.12, 63.19, 68.155: this brings out the true meaning of **comites** (line 1) as 'companions' rather than 'friends'.

15–16 The language becomes blunt and prosaic after the high poetic register of lines 1–14. The instruction to deliver a brief message is neutral, but line 16 delivers the ominous warning of what the message contains with the litotes ('not kindly words'). Referring to the lover as **meae puellae** is bitter and melancholy, recalling the happier times of 2.1, 3.3, 3.17 when she was truly 'his'.

17 The juxtaposed alliterative verbs **vivat** and **valeat** are both jussive subjunctives with a faint poignant echo of the opening line of poem 5. Just as *valete* means 'farewell', so here the phrase has the sense of 'goodbye and good luck to her'. The word **moechis** (literally, 'adulterous lovers') is postponed to the end of the line for effect. Adultery in itself is something which Catullus himself commits – if we can believe poem 68.145–6 – but, here, the nature of the girl's misbehaviour goes way beyond a single love affair as lines 18–20 make clear.

18-20 The language is monstrously hyperbolic: the girl allegedly holds (**tenet**) three hundred lovers all at once (**simul**) and reduces them repeatedly to sexual exhaustion. Such behaviour is physically implausible and reveals the poet's angry disgust more than the facts of the matter, just as **ilia rumpens** (literally, 'bursting their groins') is crude and expressive of his bitterness: note also the alliteration of **tenet trecentos** and the 'e' assonance in **vere sed identidem** enacting the repeated sexual marathons. The word **trecentos** is not to be taken literally here any more than at 9.2, 12.10 and simply means 'countless'. The final syllable of **omnium** has to elide with the opening syllable of **ilia** to allow line 19 to scan (cf. 22 below).

21-4 The poem concludes with a wistful and highly stylised stanza which is all the more striking by contrast with the crude language of 17-20.

21 **respectet** is another jussive subjunctive and has the sense of 'let her not count on my love' – i.e. 'expect to find it when she comes running back'. **ut ante** ('as previously') marks a clear break with the past.

22-4 The meaning is: '... love, which by her bad behaviour (**illius culpa**) has fallen like a flower on the furthest edge of the meadow, when it has been touched by the passing plough.' The final syllable of **prati** has to be elided with the opening vowel of **ultimi** on the next line for the line to scan, as in lines 19-20. The simile of love as a flower cut down by the plough is familiar from Sappho (fr. 105c: 'like the hyacinth on the mountains which shepherds trample on, and the purple flower is on the ground') and imitated later by Virgil (*Aeneid* 9.435-7) and it is apt that this poem in the Sapphic metre ending the relationship ends with an allusion to Sappho, just as the other poem in this metre (51) is a direct translation of Sappho. There is also a reminder of the wedding theme of the bride as a hidden flower 'unknown to the herd, torn up by no plough' (62.40) which loses all its allure once it is plucked. The imagery here places the poet in the female role of passive victim of an aggressive lover – 'ploughing' is a common metaphor for sexual conquest (e.g. Lucretius 4.1273, Sophocles *Antigone* 569, Adams *Latin Sexual Vocabulary* 154) and the final words of the poem leave us with a striking gender-reversal, whereby the male lover has been 'ploughed' by this voracious woman. Ploughs are not to blame if they hit a flower: but women are to blame if they cut down lovers. The lines show great literary finesse: notice the harsh cutting 'c' alliteration of **culpa cecidit**, the 'p' alliteration of **praetereunte postquam** and the superbly understated verb **tactus** – it only took a touch from this plough to destroy the poet's love. **culpa** reminds us that the poet complains bitterly of her bad behaviour elsewhere without losing his love for her – cf. 72, 75, 76, 85 – and that his efforts to rid himself of his feelings will not be easy, as shown in poem 8.

Poem 17

A poem addressed to a country town – possibly the poet's home town of Verona or a place nearby – which is anxious that its old bridge may not be strong enough for the festival to be played out on it. The poet proposes throwing a stupid townsman off the old bridge in order to awaken him to what his young wife is doing behind his back. The poet here (as in poem 67) is a more or less disinterested observer of the scandalous behaviour of his fellow townsmen and his language here is tame compared to the vitriol poured out against sexual misbehaviour elsewhere (e.g. for Gellius 74, 80, 88–91, on Mamurra 29, 94, on Aemilius 97). The structure of the poem is simple: the bridge (1–7), the stupid townsman (8–13) and his young wife (14–22) and the concluding repetition of the wish to throw him off the bridge (23–6).

The Roman religious office of *pontifex* (literally 'bridge-maker') was of great antiquity and importance (see *OCD* s.v. 'pontifex'), involving both religious rites and also *ludi*. The word *pons* also referred to the platform leading to the voting area in elections, and men over sixty who were ineligible to vote were 'rejected from the voting platform' (*deiecti de ponte*). Catullus may be taking this phrase literally and creating a poem around a (presumably older) husband who should be literally *deiectus de ponte*.

Roman girls as young as 12 sometimes (at least in upper-class circles) married men who were much older (see Susan Treggiari, *Roman Marriage*, pp. 398–403). Pliny, for instance, was 40 when he married his 15-year-old third wife Calpurnia. Nowhere in this poem is the husband's age mentioned but his wife is certainly young: she is a **puella** (14–15) in the flower of her youth (14) and more frisky than a young kid (15).

The variation of language is striking: the filthy mud, for instance, is **palude** (4, 10), **lutum** (9), **vorago** (11, 26), **caeno** (25). The poet makes good use of similes to describe the dolt of a husband (a baby: 12–13, a log: 18–19), his stubborn stupidity (like a horseshoe 25–6) and his flirtatious wife (tender grapes and a young kid: 15–16). The poem sets up a neat link between the bridge and the man (both feeble and unfit for purpose): the bridge has 'legs' (3) which are rickety, and it might fall flat (4) just as the man deserves to do (8–11). The poet makes use of superlatives in the central part of the poem to add intensity to the drama: the mud is **lividissima** (11), the man is **insulsissimus** (12) and his wife's charm is 'as fresh as anything' (**viridissimo** (14)) as she is to be cherished more carefully than 'the darkest (**nigerrimis**) grapes' (16).

The form of the metre of this poem is unique in the surviving poems of Catullus and is extremely rare in Latin, although poems 34 and 61 are very close. The rhythm ('Priapean') is associated with the god of male fertility Priapus, which is appropriate for this poem seeking to arouse the sexually inadequate townsman.

1–2 A **colonia** was a town, often inhabited by Roman soldiers who had served their time in the military. Equally, the word may be a proper name *Colonia*, and has been identified with Cologna Veneta, twenty miles away from Verona. This **colonia** is personified as having the wishes (**cupis**) of its townsfolk to **ludere** ('enjoy itself': cf. line 17n.) on a long bridge – along with the fears (**vereris**) of it going wrong.

2 **salire paratum habes** is an idiomatic way of saying, 'you are ready to dance' (literally, 'you have dancing prepared'). **salire** helps both to picture the festival as one involving dancing (see 6n.) and also to explain why the old bridge may not be up to it.

2-3 The bridge is now downgraded with the diminutive **ponticuli** ('poor little bridge') and its timbers (**axulis**) are **redivivis** ('second-hand', 'recycled'). **inepta** (from *in-aptus* ('ill-fitting')) is applied to the 'legs' of the bridge but it also helps to build up the image of the man being mocked here as the word *ineptus* more commonly means 'foolish, silly' – compare the use of *ineptire* at 8.1 and *ineptiarum* in 6.14.

4 **ne** + subjunctive is expressing the town's fear 'that it (the bridge) might go . . .'. **cavaque in palude** gives us the image of the bridge being swallowed up in the 'hollow' marsh.

5 The poet prays that 'a good bridge might be made for you (**tibi**) just as you desire (**ex tua . . . libidine**)'. **sic** here means 'on this condition' and looks ahead to the commands conveyed in the imperative **da** in line 7: it amounts to a conditional ('may you have a bridge if (and only if) you give me . . .').

6 The word **Salisubsalus** only occurs here in Latin. *OLD* tells us it is 'apparently a cult title, perhaps of Mars': presumably relating to the *Salii*, the 'jumping' priests of Mars, whose ritual involved dancing energetically while carrying the *ancilia* (Rome's sacred shields). **vel** shows that if 'even' the rites of Salisubsalus could be undertaken on it, then it will be strong enough for anything.

7 **maximi risūs** is a descriptive genitive going with **munus** ('a favour, one of enormous laughter'). **munus** can also mean 'spectacle' (such as the Roman games) and this sense is also prominent here as the ducking of the cuckold will be a source of public entertainment. The repetition of the vocative **Colonia** (from line1) is good ring composition to close this first section of the poem.

8-9 Translated simply, 'I want (**volo**) a fellow townsman of mine to go (**ire**) head first (**praecipitem**) from your bridge.' The term **municipem** strongly suggests that the victim is from Verona. The final 'o' of **volo** is

AS

short here as in other places where Catullus uses the word without eliding it (cf. 6.16, 17.23, 35.5, 61.209) and seems to reflect the way this word was pronounced by him.

9 The hapless man's falling (**praecipitem . . . per caputque pedesque**) frames the central word **lutum** (mud): the phrase **per caputque pedesque** ('head over heels') sounds like a colloquialism but is not found elsewhere and seems to intensify the meaning of **praecipitem** ('head first'); the polysyndeton helps to lengthen his fall into the water.

10–11 **verum** here means 'but only' and **ut** means 'where', as in 11.3: the poet is stipulating that it must not be just any mud, but that part which is 'darkest and deepest' of the entire swamp. Note how the simple word **lutum** here is first broadened by **totius lacus . . . putidae paludis** ('of the whole pool and the foul/stinking marsh') and then made more specific by the powerful superlatives **lividissima maximeque profunda**. *lividus* means properly 'greyish-blue' in colour and is the colour of the underworld pools in Virgil *Aeneid* 6.320. **vorago** means 'an abyss' and has the sense of a gaping chasm which is 'voracious' in swallowing this townsman.

12–13 **instar** + genitive means 'as much as'. *insulsus* (used of Varus' girlfriend at 10. 33) is a generalised insult ('he is an **insulsissimus** man') made more vivid by the one-line description of the **puer** as 'a two-year-old asleep on the rocking arm of his father'. The insult thus becomes increasingly extreme: he is a man (**homo**) but lacks the brains of a boy (**pueri**) who is, in fact, a toddler (**bimuli**). **tremula** is a nice touch, giving added vividness to the image with the suggestion of rocking the child to sleep, while choosing the father (rather than the mother) for this image adds to the sense of male strength and protection which is lacking in this poem of male weakness and neglect.

14 The man has not got the brains of a **puer** but he has a **puella** for a wife, and the key word **puella** is repeated in epanalepsis in 15. **cum** (+ subjunctive) and here means 'although' and **viridissimo flore** is a descriptive ablative going with the girl ('with the freshest flower', i.e. 'in the prime of youth').

14–16 The imagery varies nicely, from the concept of a bride as a flower (developed at 62.39–47) to that of a kid and, finally, that of grapes. In all cases, the adjectives supply the hyperbole: the flower is **viridissimo**, the kid is **tenellulo** and the grapes are **nigerrimis**. **tenellulo** is the affectionate diminutive of *tenellus*, which is itself a diminutive of *tener*, and softens the kid to being a sweet young pet, albeit one with a reputation for sexual forwardness (cf. Horace *Odes* 3.13.4–5). *delicatus* means 'wanton, frisky' as at 50.3.

16 Goats may misbehave, but grapes do not – and so, comparing the girl to them throws the blame onto the neglectful husband. The point of **nigerrimis** is that these grapes are fully ripe and need protecting from damage or theft.

17 **ludere** means 'to play' (as at line 1) but *ludo* and *ludus* are commonly used of sexual activity (61.204, 68.17, 99.1, Cicero *pro Caelio* 42, OLD s.v. 'ludus' 1d). **sinit** assumes (correctly in Roman times) that the husband had the power and the responsibility to ensure his wife's good behaviour – the emperor Augustus would later penalise the husbands of errant wives as being their pimps. **ut lubet** means 'as she pleases' and the idiomatic phrase *pili facere* (see 10.13n.) is intensified by **uni**, which is a variant form of the genitive of *unus* – he cares 'not a single' jot.

18–22 The dopy husband is brilliantly described in imagery of a piece of timber, supporting the idea that he is physically inert and mentally dead – as is the bridge.

18 **nec se sublevat** means 'he does not stir himself', with the suggestion that he does not arouse himself sexually for her. **ex sua parte** means 'for his part' as at 87.4, with the word **parte** adding to the sexual hint of **sublevat** (see Adams, *The Latin Sexual Vocabulary*, 45).

18–19 The log is one of **alnus** (alder tree) for good poetic reasons – Virgil tells us (*Georgics* 2.110) that these trees grow in *crassis paludibus* ('rank swamps'): and so the husband is compared to the sort of timber to be found in the sort of marsh the poet is throwing him into. This tree has been **suppernata** ('hamstrung') – a nice metaphor from warfare which reminds us that it is a human being who is being referred to – which makes the simile more complex as now the man is 'like a log' which is itself 'like a hamstrung man'. The axe is a 'Ligurian' axe as Liguria was a part of Italy which was heavily forested and where woodcutters were adept. The image is loosely based on a simile in Homer (*Iliad* 4.482–7) but Catullus ensures that the Italian colour reinvents the passage as his own.

20 The log sees everything as much as if it were not there: in other words, it sees nothing. For **nulla** used in this way, cf. 8.14. **tantundem** is the neuter accusative of *tantusdem* used here with adverbial force (see *OLD* s.v. 'tantusdem' 3) meaning 'to the same extent as if . . .'.

21–2 'That's what that man – my (model of) stupidity – is like'. The stupidity is captured in the emphatic repetitions here of **nil . . . nihil** and **sit . . . sit . . . sit . . . nescit** and in the paradoxical conceit that he is even ignorant of his own existence. **qui** here serves for *quis*.

23 The poet returns to the main premiss with a reminder of lines 8–9: **pronum** recalls **praecipitem** and the mild **ire** (9) becoming a more purposeful **mittere** here.

24 **si pote** here means '[to see] if he is able'. **repente excitare** are juxtaposed for effect – the **stolidum . . . veternum** ('dull-witted sloth') is shattered with the sudden awakening.

25 The poet wishes to throw the man **pronum** so as to leave his **supinum animum** in the mud. **supinum** here is metaphorical and means 'passive' or 'sluggish' (*OLD* s.v. 'supinus' 5), unlike line 4 where the word kept its literal meaning of 'flat on one's back'.

25–6 The poem ends with a fine simile of a mule leaving its shoe stuck in the mud: Roman mules and horses did not have metal shoes nailed into the hoof but rather leather shoes with metal soles which might well come away in muddy ground which 'clings' to it (**tenaci**). The simile reinforces the idea of the doltish husband as a mule, just like Lesbia's husband in 83.3. The simile would not have worked so well with a horse: the mule is so much more appropriate to the stubborn, infertile, unattractive fool, cf. 97.8.

Poem 34

A hymn to the goddess Diana, put into the mouths of 'unmarried boys and girls', and similar to poems 61 and 62 as being choral rather than personal lyric: this ode is asking for help for the Roman state rather than any individual favour. Diana was the Roman equivalent of the Greek goddess Artemis, sister of Phoebus Apollo, and was a virgin deity with especial links to hunting and childbirth. After one stanza introducing the god and the chorus, the poem follows the typical prayer formula: one stanza describing the parentage and birth of the god and then three on her power ('you can do so much for people when you choose') and a final stanza containing the prayer itself. There is no evidence to suggest that the poem was written for public performance.

The metre is like that of the wedding hymn 61 and is an extended form of that used in 17: three 'glyconic' lines followed by one 'pherecratean' line. The structure of the hymn is marked by features such as the tricolon of descriptive sentences beginning **tu** (lines 13–20) and the detailed reference to all aspects of the goddess' nature and activity. The poem alludes to Diana's parentage (5–6) and her birth (7–8), her different spheres of influence (9–12) and her range of titles (13–16) as she fills the farmer's barns with crops (17–20). After all this, the ending may seem somewhat anticlimactic: this goddess who can work such magic is simply asked to 'preserve the race of Romulus'.

The form of 'cletic hymn' praising and asking a divinity for help is Greek (Pindar and Callimachus being expert practitioners of the genre: see *OCD* s.v. 'Hymns, Greek') but the content here is largely Italian, culminating in a prayer for the race of Romulus.

1–3 Dianae in fide means 'under the care of Diana'; **integri** ('unsullied' or 'virgin') reminds us that the young and unmarried were especially suited to her worship as she was a virgin goddess.

4 canamus is a jussive subjunctive ('let us sing').

**A
Level**

5-6 Latona (the Greek goddess Leto) slept with the god Jupiter and gave birth to Apollo and Diana on the island of Delos. The greatness of Diana is well brought out by the repetition **maximi/magna**.

8 **deposivit** (i.e. *deposuit*) means 'dropped' in the sense of 'gave birth to'. The verb is more commonly used of animals rather than humans.

9 **fores** is the alternative form of *esses* (imperfect subjunctive of *sum*) in a purpose clause after **ut**.

10-12 The poet lists four of the domains where Diana rules (mountains, woods, glades and rivers) in an incantatory sequence of genitive nouns and adjectives. Three of the four domains are given apt and varied descriptions: their colour (**virentium**), their location (**reconditorum**) and their sound (**sonantum**). The genitive plural of the present participle of *sonare* is usually *sonantium* but **sonantum** is metrically preferable, especially in dactylic verse (e.g. Virgil *Aeneid* 6.432). The 'hypermetric' final syllable of **reconditorum** elides with the opening vowel of the next line, as does the end of line 22.

13-16 Diana is involved in childbirth and she is addressed as (**es dicta**) Juno **Lucina** in this arena. There was a temple to Juno Lucina on the Cispian Hill from 375 BC and this deity was linked to Diana also in Virgil (*Eclogues* 4.10). It was common for ancient prayers to list a variety of names for a god to ensure that the god heard the prayer, and the poet later (21-22) adds the catch-all phrase ('by whatever name it pleases you ...'). **dolentibus ... puerperis** is dative of the agent after **es dicta** ('you are called ... by women giving birth who are in pain').

15-16 Diana is now linked to Hecate as goddess of the crossroads (**Trivia**) and the moon (**Luna**). The moon's light is 'borrowed' or 'illegitimate' (**notho** is a transliteration of the Greek word for 'bastard') as it is drawn from the sun, as pointed out by Lucretius (5.575-6). Note the reinforcing juxtaposition of **lumine Luna**.

17-20 Translate: 'you, goddess, measuring (**metiens**) the yearly journey with your monthly course, fill up (**exples**) the farmer's country buildings with good crops'. The time-words **menstruo** and **annuum** fall at the end of successive lines, and there is effective repetition of sounds in **menstruo metiens iter**, suggesting the rhythm of the lunar and solar cycles. The original Roman calendar was lunar and, before 45 BC, it was 'lunisolar' rather than strictly solar.

19-20 Diana's activity as moon goddess could be seen to promote the movement of the heavenly bodies which provides crops in due season, as suggested in Virgil *Georgics* 1.5–6, Horace *Odes* 4.6.37–40. The word **rustica** seems to be unnecessary (farmers are always on agricultural land) but here introduces agriculture whereas earlier literature (e.g. *Homeric Hymn* 27, Callimachus *Hymn* 3) linked Diana/Artemis exclusively with mountains, woods and hunting (cf. 9–12). **tecta** denotes 'barns' here.

21-2 **sis** is a jussive subjunctive ('may you be **sancta**'). **placet** is the impersonal form of the verb *placeo* ('by whatever name it pleases you <to be called>').

22-4 **Romuli** is to be taken with **gentem** and the final hypermetric **-que** has to be elided with the *a-* of the first word of the following line. **antique ut solita es** means 'as you were accustomed in the old days'. Romulus was the mythical founder of Rome.

23-4 **sospites** is the present subjunctive of the archaic verb *sospito*, used in a jussive sense ('may you preserve'). **bona ope** is an instrumental ablative ('with good help'), picking up the theme of 'goodness' from **bonis** (19).

A
Level

Poem 40

A warning to a certain Ravidus (if the name is transmitted correctly) to stay away from the poet's beloved (**meos amores**) or face the consequences in the form of a poetic execution; the details of Ravidus' offence are not clarified until the last line. The tone is one of confident self-assurance, even arrogance: Ravidus must be mad to attempt this seduction unless he were seeking the sort of immortality which being lampooned in Catullus' verses would confer. The poem is made up of five indignant questions, followed by the poet's stark reply in the form of a confident future indicative (**eris**) promoted to the start of the line and followed by a pause for extra effect, followed by a witty innuendo to close. The poem as a whole is ironic: it describes and enacts the power of poetry itself, a self-fulfilling text whose promised vengeance is delivered in the promise itself.

The earlier Greek poet Archilochus was well known for 'iambic' poetry such as this (see Introduction) and his fragment 88 (= fr.172 West) is similar to this poem: 'Who has driven you mad? you will be a rich source of mockery to the people'.

Metre: hendecasyllables.

1   **quaenam** (from *quisnam*) is a stronger form of the interrogative relative – 'what, tell me . . .'. **mala mens** (as at 15.14 in a similar context) probably means 'infatuation' and is reinforced by the pitying diminutive **miselle** ('lovesick little man'). **Ravide** needs to be pronounced *Raude* for the line to scan: not a difficult pronunciation given that Latin 'v' was pronounced like a 'w'.

2   Ravidus is a passive victim of his deranged mind which 'drives him headlong' into the poet's invective. **iambos** properly refers to the iambic metre which was commonly used by earlier poets for invective poetry (see *OCD* s.v. 'Iambic poetry, Greek'): here (as at 36.5, 54.6) it stands for the poetic attack itself.

3   The second proposed explanation is that a god is behind the quarrel – an explanation which recalls, e.g., Agamemnon's account of his quarrel with Achilles in Homer *Iliad* 19.86–90. **non bene advocatus** means something like 'unwisely/improperly invoked' and suggests that Ravidus has angered a god with his botched invocation: the god avenges the slight to his authority by inducing foolish passion, on the thinking that 'those whom the gods wish to destroy – they first drive them mad' as in Sophocles *Antigone* 620–623. **tibi** operates as both dative of agent with **advocatus** and also as dative of (dis)advantage with **excitare rixam**.

4 The line is framed by the key words **vecordem . . . rixam**: **vecordem** recalls **mala mens** (1).

5 **an ut** ('or was it so that ...?') introduces alternative motives for Ravidus' behaviour. 'Reaching the mouths of the people' recalls Ennius' boast that by his verse he 'flew living through men's mouths (*per ora virum*)', suggesting that Ravidus is desperate for fame of any sort – as line 6 makes clear.

6 **quid vis?** expresses annoyed impatience and **qualubet** (i.e. *qualubet* as at 76.14, meaning 'by any means you like') adds to the tone of frustration.

7–8 The future indicative **eris**, promoted to the start of the line, and the elevated term **quandoquidem** (cf. 101.5) show the poet's self-assurance. **meos amores** means 'my darling' (as at 6.16, 10.1, 15.1, 45.1, 64.27) and refers to either gender: here it may refer to Lesbia or Iuventius (or somebody else). **cum longa ... poena** ends the poem with an innuendo: Ravidus' actions were made 'at the risk of long-lasting punishment' but the final word **poena** also suggests *pene* ('penis'). Poem 15 is a poem on a similar theme and ends with eye-watering punishments proposed for the Aurelius, who (like Ravidus) attempted to seduce the poet's beloved.

Poem 62

This and poem 61 are two wedding songs, a genre known as the *epithalamium* and also recreated in the song of the Fates in 64.323–81. Poem 62 has two separate choruses of unmarried girls and young men who are roughly the same age as the bride (**aequales**: 11, 32) engaging in a sung debate about marriage – a 'singing competition' form known as 'amoebean' as their words echo and 'cap' each other and the whole poem becomes a contest of wits, argument and linguistic ingenuity – a form found also in other poetry such as pastoral (Theocritus 5, Virgil *Eclogues* 3 and 7) and also in the amatory exchange of Horace *Odes* 3.9. The unmarried girls present marriage as threatening while the young men seek to overturn their objections with more positive imagery, in a poetic form of traditional male bravado versus female coy reluctance. The wedding hymn was a genre which others had attempted (Sappho) and which at least one (Calvus) of Catullus' contemporaries also undertook.

We do not have a huge amount of evidence on Roman weddings, but some elements are clear: the *deductio* ('leading down') of the bride from the house of her father to the house of her new husband, the veil (*flammeum*), the flaming torches (*taedae*),the *cena* (wedding feast) and the often ribald *fescennina iocatio* (teasing banter, somewhat in the manner of a best-man's speech in a modern wedding reception). Trying to apply poem 62 to a 'real' wedding is not easy – scholarly opinion is divided on whether the meal takes place, for instance, at the bride's house or the new bridegroom's house – and it is arguable that the poet intended us to read the text as a free-standing poetic work rather than an occasional poem to accompany a real wedding. Catullus puts the stage directions (e.g. 8–9) and the preparations before singing (1–19) into the finished poem, which is thus a poem about (and containing) a performance rather than simply a record of the text to be performed. The 'stage directions' do help us to some extent: the time is evening (**Vesper adest** 1), while **iam pingues linquere mensas** (3) suggests that the feast has finished, **iam veniet virgo** (4) shows that the bride is yet to arrive in the room, although the final section assumes that she is (at least by then) within earshot. The feast, in both Greece and Rome, was held in the home of the bride's parents, with boys and girls carefully segregated in Greece but not in Rome, while the wedding feast in Greece always included the bridegroom: Roman custom had the bridegroom leave the feast in order to await the *deductio* (formal procession) of his new wife into his house. The feast may be in the bride's family house: the bride has perhaps been reclining on the same couch as her bridegroom (as did Livia and Octavian, according to Dio (48.44.3)) and has now left the table to prepare for the *deductio*, perhaps to bid farewell to her mother. The groom has gone on ahead to welcome his bride to their new home. Lines 1–6 assume that preparations are in place for the *deductio* to begin. It is easier to imagine this poem being sung as the *deductio* is about to start rather than have it being sung at the bridegroom's house; there seems little doubt that the poet has chosen the moment just after the feast but just before the *deductio* of the bride, this being the very last moment when such a poem could be sung before it is all too late. So, we have a Greek/Roman wedding feast, followed by a Roman *deductio*, a Greek genre employed with Roman content.

The female chorus are obviously going to lose the contest if the wedding is to take place, but they are gallantly regarded by the young men as better prepared (11–16) and no easy opponent to vanquish (11). The contest is about the value of virginity, and the girls use a range of powerful rhetorical touches, detailed in the commentary. The women allude (46–7) to the 'double standard', whereby the virgin is sought by the ardent youths, but is less attractive to these same boys once she has become 'damaged goods' and their words are poignant and effective. The young men, however, have some good arguments and can point to marriage as desirable and attractive (look at the lovely imagery of fire and light in 26–30), happy and ordained by the gods (30), and a vital part of the social fabric, as the language of commitment brings out in 27–8, and the drooping vine needs to be 'married' to a tree to thrive. The women may even agree secretly (**ficto ... questu** 36). The male

A
Level

arguments may be pitched against what Wiseman well calls 'the beauty of innocence' but they have a good deal of beauty of their own. Their stanzas have rhetorical vigour and this rebuts their own ironical casualness as they hear the girls rehearse (12). The final words addressed to the bride are both admonitory and also reassuring: your parents love you, have invested in your future with a dowry (65) and will therefore have chosen well for you; and it is better not to fight against your family both old and new. It is important, however, not to take the lines too seriously. The occasion is a happy one and the emotions are to a large extent the ones expected without being wholly serious. People do, after all, cry at weddings without being unhappy.

The structure of the poem is as follows:

1–5   Young men talk among themselves (5 lines)

6–10 Young women talk among themselves (5 lines)

11–19 Young men prepare to sing (9 lines)

20–25 Young women's first stanza (6 lines)

26–31 Young men's first stanza (6 lines)

32ff Young women's second stanza (lacuna in ms – originally 7 lines)

33–38 Young men's second stanza (originally 7 lines)

39–48 Young women's third stanza (11 lines – assuming a lacuna after 41)

49–58 Young men's third stanza (11 lines)

59–66 Young men address the bride

1 **Vesper** (the evening star) is the planet Venus when it rises at twilight. **consurgite**: the young men are reclining in typical Roman style on couches while enjoying the wedding feast. They are in a position to see the sky, whereas the women cannot (see line 7). **Olympo** is the mountain in Greece said to be the abode of the gods, here standing for 'the heavens', the gods' terrestrial home standing for their celestial dwelling. The word is in a locative ablative case ('on Olympus'), but the juxtaposition of **Vesper Olympo** creates the pleasing image of the star seeming to rise from the top of the mountain. The word also keeps the divine presence firmly in mind right from the start of the wedding hymn.

2 The young men are impatient. The light has been awaited for a long time (**expectata diu**) and the star is 'only just now' rising after all this time (**vix tandem**), with the key term **lumina tollit** left to the end of the line – delayed in verse as in life.

3–4 The fourfold repetition of **iam** is effective and metrically varied, with the first and third falling on the stressed first syllable of the foot, while the second and fourth fall on the unstressed second part of the foot. The pattern of infinitive + **iam**: **iam** + infinitive in line 3 is a neat chiasmus, whereas line 4 has a balanced repetition. **tempus** + infinitive understands *est* to mean 'it is time to …', whereas in 4 the adverb **iam** means 'any moment now' (cf. 18).

4 **Hymenaeus** is the title of the formal wedding song. The final syllable of **dicetur** is lengthened before **Hymenaeus**, a usage which seems to have been common before this particular word (cf. 64.20, Virgil *Aeneid* 7.398, 10.720). The term **Hymenaeus** for the refrain uttered at a Greek wedding is as old as Homer (*Iliad* 18.493) and came to stand for the wedding song itself (as here), and by synecdoche for the idea of marriage as a whole (where it is usually plural as at 64.20).

5 **Hymen O Hymenaee** is a ritual cry uttered at points in the poem where there is a change of speaker. The poet varies the quantity of the first syllable of **Hymen**, whereby it is scanned long (*Hȳmen*) in the nominal form and short in the adjectival form (*Hўmenaee*) – exactly as Theocritus (*Idyll* 18.58) does in his wedding song for Helen and Menelaus.

6–10 The unmarried women (**innuptae**) now rise, to match the boys' song in reply (**contra**) and to be seen as superior (see line 9). Their language mirrors that of the boys: **Vesper** becoming **Noctifer**, **lumina tollit** becoming **ostendit … ignes**, Mt Olympus is matched by Mt Oeta.

7 The word **nimirum** usually indicates that the speaker is inferring something which cannot be known; here, the girls cannot see the evening star themselves from deep within the dining hall, but they infer its rising from the behaviour of the boys (who are seated where they can see the sky).

Oetaeos: Mt Oeta was in southern Thessaly in Greece. Hercules was famously cremated on this mountain and so the term 'Oetaean fires' could have recalled this 'implicit myth' in the reader (cf. 24n, and also 68.115–16, where Hercules' own marriage to Hebe is mentioned) – but these 'Oetaean fires' are, in fact, the rays of Venus. The ancient commentator Servius (writing on Virgil *Eclogues* 8.30) tells us that there was a cult of Hesperus the evening star on Mount Oeta. **Noctifer** ('bringer of night') is not found in Latin before Catullus and was possibly invented by him on the model of *Lucifer* for the morning star: it also makes for a pleasing oxymoron as the bringer of darkness shows fires.

8   sic certe est ('Yes, that is it') shows that they now regard the inference (**nimirum**) in line 7 to be valid. **viden** is the contracted form for *videsne* ('do you see?', cf. 61.77) and the phrasing of **sic certe est; viden ut** gives a colloquial tone to the line. **ut** here means 'how' but (as in 12 and 61.77) it is followed by the indicative, not the subjunctive normal in indirect questions. **exsiluere** is the shortened form of the perfect form *exsiluerunt*.

9   non temere suggests some nervous anticipation from the women as they face men who (they say) would not have stood up without good cause. **par** essentially means 'equal' but here has the sense of 'fair, reasonable' (*OLD* s.v. 'par' 14) while keeping the overtone of 'well matched' as below at 57.

11–18   The young men also panic slightly: the girls have been working on their song while the men have been otherwise engaged. This sounds like an attempt to excuse defeat in advance by accepting that the girls deserve to win.

11   palma (a palm branch) was the sign of a victor in chariot-racing and came to indicate other victories such as securing the favours of a girl (Ovid *Amores* 3.2.82 plays on the two senses). The competitive imagery of rivalry between the genders appears to undercut any notion of marital harmony at this stage – a rivalry which is only put aside at the end of the poem (59). **parata** here denotes 'ready to hand' and there is a pleasing jingle of **pār est . . . parata est.**

12 aspicite . . . ut picks up **viden ut** from 8. **meditata requirunt** ('they are recalling what they have rehearsed') shows that the men realise that the women have planned their performance, in contrast to their own extempore performance. *meditor* is deponent but the perfect participle here is passive in sense. **secum** (literally 'with themselves') means 'among themselves'.

13 non frustra picks up **non temere** from line 9. The line is elegant, with two verbs juxtaposed in the centre.

14 penitus . . . tota . . . laborant nicely conveys the girls' intense efforts, while the *e-i-u* assonance of **nec mirum penitus** makes us question the men's protestations of their own inferiority.

15 The line is elegant with anaphora of **alio** and a balanced antithesis of **mentes** and **aures**. The point being made in **alio . . . alio** is that they have not paid attention to their song but allowed themselves to be distracted – possibly by the food.

16 'we will rightly be defeated': a touch of honesty and sportsmanship, explained by the sententious gnomic phrase **amat victoria curam.** The men may lose the contest but they are retaining their dignity.

17 nunc alerts them to the need for urgent action and **animos convertite** nicely counters line 15 with a call for concentration. The force of **nunc . . . saltem** is, 'you have not done much so far but you could *at least* try *now*'.

18 The line is balanced around the caesura, with each half containing **iam** + infinitive + verb in varied order. **dicere** here (as at line 5) means 'to sing'.

20-5 The girls begin with a frightening account of marriage from their virginal viewpoint. They see marriage as rape: the bride's virginity and security are plundered. The imagery of fire and fury runs through the stanza: the star is an **ignis**, the youth is ablaze with passion (**ardenti**), and the image of the sacked (and presumably torched) city accords well with this. The concept of marriage as ritualised rape was memorialised in the ritual of the spear (*hasta caelibaris*) used to part the bride's locks, a notion going back to the rape of the Sabine women (cf. Ovid *Fasti* 2.560, Treggiari *Roman Marriage* 163).

20   fertur (passive of *fero*) here means 'travels' and **caelo** is local ablative ('in the sky').

21-2 The cruelty is vivid, with repetition of **complexu avellere matris/complexu matris . . . avellere** and chiastic repetition of **natam . . . matris . . . matris . . . natam**. The juxtaposition of **retinentem avellere** enacts the image of the girl hanging on to (**retinentem**) her mother while the wicked Hesperus 'tears' her 'away'. The subjunctive **possis** is explanatory ('<seeing that you are> one who could . . .').

23 The outrage here is emphasised by the juxtaposition **ardenti castam** – if she were not **castam** and/or if he were not **ardenti**, the situation would be less traumatic for the girl.

24 The stanza ends with **crudelius** picking up **crudelior** from line 20. Girls were raped and abducted when cities were sacked: compare the sacking of Oechalia and capture of the beautiful Iole by Hercules (as in Sophocles' *Trachiniae* and Ovid *Heroides* 9), and the way in which Briseis describes being taken captive by Achilles after the slaughter of her husband and the capture of her city (Homer *Iliad* 19.295–300). The most iconic example of such brutal plundering of women was the sacking of Troy, where ladies such as Andromache were taken (cf. Virgil *Aeneid* 3.323–7 and Euripides' play *Trojan Women*).

26-30 Line 26 is as close as possible to line 20, but the tiny changes indicate a totally different stance. The men argue that marriage is *iucundus* rather than *crudelis*: the same event (marriage), just now seen

A Level

from the point of view of female victims, is now cast in a more positive light. They switch focus from rape to harmony: the agreement between the husband and the parents of the girl (enhanced by the balanced phrasing of 28), the glorious light of the star, and marriage as a state of happiness greater than any other given by the gods (30), a vision of felicity enhanced by the reinforcing juxtaposition of **felici optatius**. As with the previous stanza, 'fire' imagery is prominent: **ignis ... flamma ... ardor.**

27–9   **desponsă** and **cōnūbiă** go together ('pledged wedding') together and **tuā** goes with **flammā**. The marriage has already (**ante**) been pledged at betrothal (*sponsio*), when the father and the prospective husband of the bride both undertook the commitment of marrying the bride to the groom (*pactio nuptialis*, here referred to with the verb **pepigere**), but they have not completed the agreement (**iunxere**) until now when the evening star rises.

28   The repetition and plosive alliteration of **pepigere ... pepigerunt** underlines the formality of the betrothal ceremony and suggests the legally binding status, just as the repetition in lines 21–2 stressed the cruelty of the process. Understand **quae** as picking up **conubia** from 27.

29   **ardor** recalls the metaphorical 'burning' (**ardenti**) of the passionate young bridegroom in line 23 and the term possibly alludes to the need for the bridegroom's passion to effect the union (in contrast to the impotent bridegroom in poem 67.21–2).

30   'What is given by the gods more desirable than the hour of bliss?' **felici hora** is an ablative of comparison. Once again, this line caps the girls' line 24, with the emphasis here on the *good* fortune of being married, reinforced by the conjunction of **felici optatius** and the reference to the gods (themselves a byword for bliss). Achilles, for example, in Homer's *Iliad* (24.525–33) tells Priam that the gods dispense bad fortune as well as good but that they themselves are happy.

A Level

32 The girls address each other as **aequales** ('comrades') as the boys did in 11.

32-3 The poem is symmetrically composed with each of the two choruses having a roughly equal amount of space: however, the text here jumps from the first line of a girls' stanza to the middle of a boys' stanza: there is clearly a gap (of at least the rest of the girls' stanza and the beginning of the boys') in the manuscripts at this point; the scribe may have confused *Hesperus* in line 31 with a later line also beginning *Hesperus* and omitted what came between them. We can infer the content of the lost stanza, however, from the wording of the 'reply' at lines 33-7, and Goold conjectures that the missing lines were something like:

> namque suo adventu fert omnibus ille pericla;
> nocte timent cuncti, nisi quos aliena petentes,
> Hespere, tu radiis properas accendere blandis.
> at libet iniusta pueris te extollere laude.
> quid tum, si laudant, sibi mox quem quisque timebunt?
> Hymen o Hymenaee Hymen ades o Hymenaee!
>
> Hespere, te innuptae nunc falso crimine laedunt:

('for at his coming he brings danger to everybody; by night everybody is afraid, except those who are seeking to steal other people's property, whom you, evening star, hasten to spur on with your soft beams. Boys like to acclaim you with undeserved praise: what does their praise matter, if soon they will all be fearing you? O Hymenaeus Hymen, come, O Hymenaeus Hymen. Evening star, the girls are stinging you with a false charge.')

33 The boys reply to the girls' accusation (that night is a time for thieves) by stating that, in fact, the star is one who *catches* thieves as his rising is the sign for the watchmen to work.

34-5 Venus, the star which brings night and (the girls claim) allows thieves to hide, also regularly appears as the morning star, with name changed to **Eous** ('star of dawn'), and catches these same burglars still burgling when he returns (**revertens**). Line 35 is elegant, with the two names for the same star framing the line, the verb **comprendis** (the short form of *comprehendis*) central and **mutato . . . nomine** balanced on either side.

36–7 The boys allege that the girls are faking their distaste and are eager for marriage but dare not say so (**tacita mente**), cf. 66.16. The construction is as follows: the impersonal verb **lubet** with **innuptis** in the dative ('it is pleasing to the unmarried (girls)') is followed by the infinitive **carpere** ('to criticise').

39–47 The girls assert that virginity is precious – as soon as she has lost her 'flower', a girl will be shunned. The poet uses the metaphor of the flower of virginity and turns it into a simile of remarkable skill and beauty.

39–44 The lines make good use of variety of phrasal length. 39 is complete in itself, while 40, 42 and 44 are all divided into two phrases at the caesura, and line 41 contains three balanced phrases of verb + subject. The heavy spondees of lines 39 and 41 well evoke the slow process of maturation. The three verbs in line 41 are well chosen: **mulcent** suggests the comforting of an infant, **firmat** suggests the strengthening of the growing limbs, while **educat** brings the process to completion as the child/flower is brought to maturity: we have here the soothing breezes, the power of the sun and the nurturing rainfall.

39–40 The exclusivity of the flower is stressed: it is in an 'enclosed' (**saeptis**) garden and is known to no animate thing. The plural **hortis** adds a touch of grandeur. **ignotus** is a nice elliptical touch – if the flocks knew of the flower, they would chew it and so the word also suggests 'safety'. The violence of the flower's possible fate is conveyed with the strong word **convulsus** (from *convellere*, picking up *avellere* from lines 21–2). The image of the flower of youthful beauty and innocence is as old as Sappo (Fr. 105C LP: possibly from a wedding hymn) and Catullus himself uses it strongly at 17.14, 64.402 of vulnerable young women. The brutality of the image of a flower torn by the plough is found also

A
Level

in 11.22–4, Homer *Iliad* 8. 306f, Virgil *Aeneid* 9.435. The difference here is that this flower is *safe* from such accidents and is a delicate and protected species, like the precious virginity of the girls.

42   The two halves of the line are marked with repetition of **multi . . . multae** and parallel positioning of **pueri . . . puellae** as in line 44. **optavere** (for *optaverunt*) is the so-called 'gnomic' perfect tense, expressing a general rule rather than a particular historic instance (cf. 64.240).

43   The fragility of the flower is well evoked in the way it is plucked with even so insignificant a thing as a slender (**tenui**) fingernail. The flower loses its blooms instantly on being plucked, as is shown by the juxtaposition of **carptus defloruit**.

45   **dum** usually means 'while': here, it is used twice in a correlative phrase to mean 'for as long as (she remains untouched), for so long (is she dear . . .)', a form of phrasing which is repeated at 56. The final monosyllable makes the rhythm of the ending of this line harsh, with a clash of the metrical beat and the speech accent (**dum/cára sú/is ést**) – the strongest example of this usage in this poem.

46   A powerfully rhetorical and hyperbolic line. **amisit** has the sense of waste as well as loss, juxtaposed with idea of purity (**castum**) and followed by the sordid result (**polluto corpore**). The line mixes the two metaphors (of the 'flower' of virginity and the 'polluted body'), as well as creating the strong assonance of **corpore florem**.

47   The response of the two sexes is interestingly similar for different reasons: she is no longer *attractive* (**iucunda**) to boys and no longer *liked* by (**cara**) girls, the final phrase picking up **cara suis** from 45. Men may prefer to marry virgins but it is not obvious why a sullied girl is no longer liked by her peers, unless (perhaps) she is letting the side down and abandoning the cause of chastity, giving way to pleasures which other girls are (reluctantly) prepared to forego. It may be significant that these are the last words the women sing before they lose the contest.

**A
Level**

49-58 The boys reply forcefully: far from being a danger and a waste, marriage is a positive opportunity to flourish and grow. The language is partly that of the farmer 'marrying' the vine by making it grow on and around a supporting tree. This (as with the 'flower' metaphor above) allows the chorus to take a metaphor and develop it into a simile, complete with poetic and descriptive effects.

49 **vidua** is frequently applied to people who are single or widowed but is also the technical term for the 'unsupported' vine. **nudo** here means 'devoid of trees' but the primary sense of 'naked' reinforces the sexual imagery and enhances the image of the vulnerable unmarried woman.

50 **numquam** is emphatically repeated after the caesura (cf. lines 4, 15, 18, 28, 42, 44, 53, 55, 63) to break the line into two halves, with strong stress here on the impossibility of growth. **educat** picks up line 41, and the line ends with pleasing assonance of **educat uvam**.

51-2 The hapless plight of the limp vine unwedded to a tree and falling flat on the ground is well brought out: her body is delicate (**tenerum**) and she cannot rise as her frail stem is being bent by her own 'downward weight' (**prono ... pondere**). The vine should be stretching upwards but, in fact, is using her topmost tendril (**summum ... flagellum**) to touch the root, and the sequence of spondees in line 52 brings out the sluggish nature of the process. The phrasing is surprising: we expect her to be touching the root with her tendril and not *vice versa*, and **iam iam** has the sense of 'any moment now'. The juxtaposition of **radice flagellum** enacts the pathetic juxtaposition of the root and tendril. Line 51 is well balanced in an A–B–C–B–A pattern.

53 Oxen (**iuvenci**) were used to break up the ground around the vine to enrich the soil (cf. Virgil *Georgics* 2.356).

54 The simile returns to the theme of human marriage with the word **marito** ('as a husband'), which is also the *mot juste* for a tree which has been joined to a vine. The metaphor of agricultural 'marriage' is easily

A
Level

unpacked as literal marriage: since **ulmo** is feminine in gender, the word **marito** must be a noun in apposition rather than an adjective.

55 The transformation of the vine from drooping failure to total success (and universal approval) is conveyed in the transformation of line 53 to line 55, where with minimal change (from **nulli** to **multi**) the outlook is transformed.

56–7 The men mockingly quote the girls' words in line 45 back at them, seeing **intacta** ('untouched') as a sure route to growing old 'untended' (**inculta**), picking up the term from **coluere** of the previous line; **senescit** applies pressure on the girl to marry while she can as the alternative fate is to become an 'old maid', resented by her parents: this answers the girls' argument in 45–6 that virginity ensured their popularity with their family.

57 The second vowel of **conubium** is usually scanned long, but that is only possible here if the -*i* is consonantal and the word becomes one of three syllables (*cō/nūb/jum*) rather than four, with the final -*um* long by position before the two 'm' consonants in -*um m*-. It is more likely that the scansion of the word was a matter of choice and that Catullus here intended the vowel to be short.

57–8 The bride is 'less resented' by her father, presumably because he wants to marry her off and save himself the anxiety and expense of keeping her and planning for her future. The key phrase explaining the line is **maturo tempore** in 57: the young men are suggesting that if the girl weds earlier rather than later, she will be younger and more attractive to her husband and will have cost her father less in maintenance: and while **maturo tempore** can mean simply 'in the fullness of time', it also carries the sense of 'early' (see OLD s.v. 'maturus' 8).

59–65 The men have the last word, concluding the singing contest with advice directly to the bride, who has (one assumes) accepted that they are right to recommend marriage.

**A
Level**

59   The prohibition formed by **ne** + imperative (for the more common *noli* + infinitive found at 64 below or *ne* + perfect subjunctive) is used elsewhere by Catullus (61.193, 67.18). The men reveal their admiration for 'such a husband' (**tali coniuge**) and the union is realised by the juxtaposition of **coniuge virgo**.

60   **aequum** means 'right' or 'fair' but also has the sense of 'evenly matched' and chimes well with the argument that the girl is hopelessly outnumbered by the combined triple weight of one husband and two parents. Understand the Latin thus: 'it is not right to fight <with a man> to whom your father himself handed you over'.

61   The weight of parental authority is spelled out by the repetition in **pater ... ipse/ipse pater** before adding 'mother' and then reminding the bride that she must obey them both, allowing a faint verbal suggestion that one must *pārere* one's *părentibus*. The argument counters the girls' plaintive complaint that marriage amounts to a girl being torn from her mother's embrace (21–4).

62–4   Quinn calls this 'the argument from arithmetic': for this sort of calculating language, cf. 5.7–11, Sophocles *Antigone* 905–12.

62   The term **ex parte** means 'partly' and **parentum** is possessive genitive, so that the whole line means 'your virginity is not all your own, it is partly owned by your parents'.

63–4   The word **tertia** is used (appropriately) three times. The two parents are specified, while the bride herself is reduced to a short word of two syllables (**tua** – itself reduced by the elision with **est**), with her share 'only' (**sola**) a third.

64   The phrase **pugnare duobus** was proverbial ('even Heracles could not face two people' (Plato *Phaedo* 89c)) for a battle one could not win and here the sexual sense of 'fighting' (cf. 66.13 'the nocturnal fighting', Propertius 2.15.4) is developed into a metaphorical fight against superior forces.

A Level

65 The girl's parents have handed over their 'rights' over her, along with the dowry, to the man who is now their son-in-law (**genero**). The dowry was property transferred to the husband from the bride's parents in order to support her, and was refundable if the marriage was dissolved (see *OCD* s.v. 'Marriage Law, Roman' and Treggiari, *Roman Marriage*, pp. 323–64).

Poem 64

This is one of the few surviving examples in Latin of the miniature epic or *epyllion*, a form which dates from Alexandrian times and was favoured by poets such as Callimachus (who wrote a *Hecale*) and Moschus (*Europa*). It is epic in metre (hexameters), in its mythological subject-matter and in its poetic register, but is in other ways a far cry from Homer and Virgil. It was very popular with the New Poets of the first century BC: Cinna wrote a *Smyrna*, praised by Catullus and favourably contrasted with Volusius' *Annales* in poem 95; Calvus wrote an *Io*, Cornificius a *Glaucus*, Valerius Cato a *Dictynna*.

This is not a linear tale: the story of the marriage of Peleus and Thetis frames a 'story within a story', with more than half (216 of the 408 lines) of the poem given over to this 'digression' describing a coverlet adorning the marriage bed of the bridal couple. The whole central tableau is an example of the device known as *ecphrasis* – the set-piece description of a work of art in narrative form – found in other ancient literature such as the depiction of the Shield of Achilles (Homer *Iliad* 18. 478–613), the mantle of Jason (Apollonius Rhodius *Argonautica* 1.730–67), and later on the shield of Aeneas (Virgil *Aeneid* 8. 608–731). Catullus skilfully exploits the *ecphrasis*, playing off the physical object against the broader narrative behind it, covering his tracks with **perhibent** (124) which states that the details are from the legend as well as from the coverlet. The static coverlet is animated from the start and the poet gives us narrative details (such as the climbing of hills (126) and running into water (128)) along with the quotation of a whole speech, which, by definition, cannot be taken from the coverlet.

The story of Theseus and Ariadne is as follows: Athens was compelled to send young people every year as human sacrifices to King Minos in Crete as punishment for an earlier crime – once in Crete, they were fed to the Minotaur who lived in the Labyrinth and who was the offspring of the sexual union of the queen (Pasiphae) and a bull. Theseus had joined the group going to Crete and was determined to kill this Minotaur, but needed a means of finding his way out of the Labyrinth. King Minos' daughter Ariadne fell in love with Theseus and helped him to escape by means of a ball of wool, which he unwound on his way in and then rewound on his way back. Ariadne had thus betrayed her father and her homeland and fled with the victorious Theseus from Crete, hoping for a future life with him. They stopped at the island of Naxos, where she was abandoned by Theseus.

Only lines 124–64 are printed and discussed here, but it is important to read the whole poem in translation to appreciate what is, by any standards, a masterpiece. For further discussion of the themes of the poem, see the website accompanying this book.

The structure of the poem is as follows:

1–30 The meeting of Peleus and Thetis
31–49 The human guests arrive: description of the palace
50–264 The tapestry ecphrasis
    50–1 bridge passage
    52–70 Ariadne on the beach
    71–115 Theseus' earlier arrival in Crete: Ariadne falls in love
    116–31 bridge passage returns us to Ariadne on the beach
    132–201 Ariadne's speech
    202–14 bridge passage: Ariadne's curse prompts flashback to
        Theseus' leaving of Athens
    215–37 Aegeus' farewell speech
    238–48 Ariadne's curse fulfilled
    249–50 return to Ariadne on the beach
    251–64 Bacchus and his entourage

**A
Level**

124–31   The poet picks up the account of Ariadne on the island where he left it at line 75. She is described as climbing the steep cliffs (presumably to keep Theseus' ship in view (126–7)) and also, when it has vanished over the horizon, running into the water (128). **tum ... tum ...** does not indicate a narrative sequence of events but is more 'now this ... now that' (see *OLD* s.v. 'tum' 10).

124   perhibent ('they say') puts the story into indirect speech, distancing the poet from his tale and exchanging the ecphrastic description (of a coverlet) for a more narrative voice. Ariadne's extreme emotion is brought out by the strong cluster of words in **ardenti corde furentem. saepe** could be taken either with **perhibent** ('they often say') or with **illam** ('that she often ...'). The second option is favoured by translators, as it adds to the sense of her impatient passion.

125   The line is chiastically constructed: adjective A – adjective B – verb – noun B – noun A. **clarisonas** is a compound adjective (*clari-sonas*) and well evokes in its length the amplitude of her shouting. The term is ironic as her words, however eloquent and clear, cannot be heard by Theseus.

126–8   The tense of the infinitive moves from perfect (**fudisse**) to the more vivid present in **conscendere**. Ariadne climbs up to a vantage point to keep Theseus' ship in view for as long as possible, but what she sees is sea rather than ship, as is shown in 127 **pelagi vastos ... aestus. vastos** means 'massive' and also here the sense 'dreary' or 'endless' (see *OLD* s.v. 'vastus' 2), while the difficulty of the climb is evoked in the heavy syllables in 126. **protenderet** is subjunctive after **unde**, showing the purpose of her actions: 'from where she might direct her gaze ...'.

128 In the time between this line and the previous one, Ariadne has run from the top of the hill down to the sea. **tremuli** is elsewhere used of people (e.g. 307, 17.13, 61.51, 68.142): the reader might expect it here to apply to Ariadne shaking with anger/fear, when, in fact, it goes with **salis** ('salt' here as metonymy for 'the sea') and means 'rippling' with waves.

129 A 'Golden Line' (as at 163, 172, 242, 264) with adjective A – adjective B – verb – noun A – noun B. The poet has already (63–7) described Ariadne's clothes falling off on the beach in her mad grief (rather like Andromache in Homer *Iliad* 22.468–70), but, at this point, she is lifting her skirt to prevent it getting wet. **nudatae** sounds enticing and the body part revealed (**surae**) is teasingly postponed until the end of the line. **mollia** ('soft', 'feminine') agrees with the clothing (**tegmina**) but also applies to the wearer.

130 **maestam** recalls **tristem** (126). **extremis** focalises her state of mind and means 'desperate' (*OLD* s.v. 'extremus' 4b: cf. 169, 76.18) as she has no idea that she is going to be rescued by Dionysus (251–3).

131 **frigidulos** is a pathetic diminutive, conveying pity and affection (cf 103, 3.18): the sobbing of **singultus** and the detail of her 'wet face' (**udo ore**) combine to create a pathetic image.

132–201 Ariadne's lament: the longest section of the poem and a rhetorical *tour de force* which was imitated and admired in later ages (cf. e.g. Ovid *Heroides* 10). We might forget that the poem purports to be describing a picture on a tapestry when we read this speech in which the picture, having already gone from static image to motion picture, now utters sound as well – although the poet covers himself of any charge of inconsistency with his verb **perhibent** ('they say' 76 and 126), which points out that the poet is not (just) describing a picture but also reporting stories. The context (and some of the detail) of her lament is familiar to us already from the previous narrative, but the switch from third-person narrative to direct speech allows the poet to do several things: first, to repeat and reinforce the abandonment of Ariadne, who

A Level

is formally trapped on the coverlet as she is on the island and who in her speech breaks the generic bounds to express this isolation; second, to expand our vision of the narrative with mention of things which a picture could not convey – she recalls events in the past such as Theseus' promise of marriage (139–41) and her leaving home (180–3) and she envisages what will happen to her (e.g. being eaten by wild beasts (152–3)) as well as alternative scenarios of what could have been (160–3). The poet will later vivify the picture further with a sequence of Bacchic sounds (251–64): here, he animates the emotions and brings out the energy and passion locked inside a static imprisoned form, allowing this caged bird to sing.

132–4   The tirade begins with emphatic repetitions, first of **perfide**, then of **sicine** (i.e. *sici-ne* (as the question suffix -*ne* is added to the expanded form of *sic* – 'is this how …?')), both at key metrical points (fifth foot and first foot), as at 259–60. Ariadne claims that she has been 'abducted' (**avectam**) from her family altars to reinforce the power of **perfide**.

133   There is pleasing assonance and alliteration of l̲iquisti̲ in l̲itore: and Ariadne spits out the accused's name alliteratively in li̲tore, T̲heseu.

134   Ariadne's stress on divine powers (**aris … neglecto numine divum**) allies her with the gods (who uphold oaths) against the 'traitor' who had sworn to take her home with him (139–48, especially 146–7), and perhaps hints at Bacchus' divine help about to save her. The **numen** of a god was their power as shown in the 'nodding' of the divine head (see 204n.). **divum** is the contracted form of *divorum* ('of the gods') as at 76.4 and **neglecto numine** is an ablative absolute.

135   **immemor** ('forgetful') was the narrator's explanation in line 58 for Theseus sailing away without her, and it will come back to haunt him when (as a result of Ariadne's curse (200–1)) he 'forgets' to change the sails on his ship and causes the suicide of his father (202–50). **portas** is pointed – he should be carrying Ariadne but, in fact, the freight is one of **devota periuria** ('accursed broken oaths'). Ariadne signals the high emotion with the exclamation **a!**, a usage found at line 71 and in other poems of the period (Calvus' *Io* (Frag. 9)). The line makes strong use of 'd' and 'p' alliteration for hostile effect.

136–7   A third rhetorical question (**sicine . . . sicine . . . nullane . . .**), this time using enjambement to convey the overflow of emotion. Ariadne now sees her abandonment as an act of cold calculation – a callous (**crudelis**) mind (**mentis**) using **consilium** rather than love – and that the time for changing his mind is over (note the perfect tense **potuit**).

137–8   The sardonic tone is here evident: 'you had no **clementia** available (**praesto**) so that your harsh heart might be willing (**vellet**) to take pity on me'. **inmite pectus** recalls Cupid's *immiti corde* at line 94 – Theseus is as harsh a lover as Love himself. She also speaks with some sarcasm as she is treating as an act of compassion what was, in fact, his duty.

139–41   More rhetorical repetitions (**non haec . . . non haec . . . sed . . . sed**) as she contrasts Theseus' former promises and charming tone (**blanda voce**) with the grim present reality. The promises were also freely given (**dedisti**), not wrung from him reluctantly.

140–1   **miserae** refers to Ariadne. The dative case is surprising after **iubebas** (and the text is suspect), but **miserae** is well chosen: when he gave her hope (**sperare iubebas**), she was **miser** in the sense of 'lovesick' (cf. Lucretius 4. 1076, Propertius 1.1.1), whereas now she is **miser** in the broadest sense – in sharp contrast to the joys of **laeta . . . optatos**. There is effective chiasmus in 141 and an unusual rhythm as the line has no strong caesura and no coincidence of metrical beat and speech accent in the fifth foot (see the Introduction on the metres). Goold points out that the line can be read as two separate metrical units which form the metre used for wedding songs (such as poem 61), 'to which this is a pathetic allusion'. For the meaning of **hymenaeos**, see poem 62.4n.

142   Ariadne speaks in terms which are both literal – the sea breezes have carried him and his words far away – and metaphorical: for the

A Level

phrasing (first seen in Homer *Odyssey* 8.408–9), cf. 59, 164–5, 239–40, 30.9–10, Virgil *Aeneid* 9.312–13.

143–8 Ariadne generalises her individual experience into a castigation of all men: no longer should *any* woman trust *any* man.

143–4 Ariadne says much the same thing in different language in successive lines, with a nice jingle of **nunc iam nulla viro**, the repetition of **nulla . . . nulla** and **viro . . . viri; iuranti** picks up the 'oath' theme of **periuria** (135), and **credat** in 143 is picked up in **fideles** in the same position in 144, while **speret** picks up **sperare iubebas** (140). **credat** and **speret** are both jussive subjunctives ('let (no woman) trust') as in 5.1. **nunc** must here mean 'from now onwards'.

145–8 Men, says Ariadne, will say anything to get what they want, and then will go back on their words once their desire has been satisfied. **quīs** is the contracted form of *quibus* and refers back to the men understood from 143–4, acting as a referential or possessive dative ('while their heart desires . . .'). The generalisation is striking: these men have a singular **animus** (the appetitive side of the mind) in a state of desire (**cupiens**) which is anticipating (**prae-**) the acquisition (**apisci**) of a vague 'something' (**aliquid** – which may be sex or even (as here) success in the Labyrinth).

146 The rhetorical repetition of **nil . . . nihil** is well placed metrically, and there is a neat chiasmus of verb+infinitive – infinitive+verb, ending with scornful plosive alliteration. The two verbs are well chosen: they are not afraid (**metuunt**) to swear (when any decent man should fear to swear falsely) and they are not mean (**parcunt**) with their promises (only with actually delivering on them).

147–8 This sentence answers 145–6 in similar terms: **cupidae** picks up **cupiens**, and **mentis** picks up **animus**, there is another repetition of **nihil . . . nihil** and another use of **metuo**. Catullus seems to be using the language of sexual desire (**libido**), but Ariadne presumably feels that the sexual bond, rather than being the purpose of the lies, was rather the means by which Theseus managed to satisfy his ulterior motive of slaying the Minotaur. **metuere** is the syncopated form of *metuerunt*: the tense has to be read as 'gnomic' perfect expressing a general statement as at 62.42.

149–51 There is heavy use of elision here: five words ending with a vowel (or -*um*) run into the following word if it begins with a vowel: *cert(e) ego t(e) in . . . eripu(i) et . . . german(um) amittere . . . suprem(o) in.* This suggests the outpouring of Ariadne's emotions.

149–50 Ariadne reminds Theseus that she saved him and (in effect) killed for him, as Medea says to Jason in Euripides' *Medea* (476–87). The phrase 'in the middle of the whirlpool of death' is striking, reminding us of the simile of the **turbo** used to describe Theseus killing the Minotaur (105–9). **medio** intensifies the sense of danger, as does the expressive participle **versantem** as he is 'whirling' in danger; and her saving act (**eripui**) is emphatically postponed in enjambement to the start of the next line and the end of the phrase.

150 Ariadne here (as at 181) describes the Minotaur – the hybrid half-brother offspring of her mother Pasiphae and the bull – as her 'brother' (**germanum**). **crevi** ('I decided') sounds like a positive choice based on a calculation of profit and loss. It may seem odd for her to have affection for the Minotaur – she brings him in here as a desperate emotional argument ('I gave up my brother for you') but the matter still raises awkward questions in the reader's mind. If she is accessory to fratricide, then can she claim the moral high ground? The issue also uses the theme of human (or semi-human) sacrifice, which recurs later in the poem (especially 362–70).

151 **dessem** is a syncopated form of **de-essem** (imperfect subjunctive of *desum*). **fallaci** (deriving from *fallere*) was last used of the sleep which tricked her in 56. The juxtaposition of **fallaci supremo** here adds the dig that she helped him at a critical time and yet he still cheated her.

152–3 A familiar terror in the ancient world is that of one's corpse lying unburied – both the fear of the soul not reaching the underworld and the horror of the body being eaten by birds and animals; cf. Homer

Iliad 1.4–5, Sophocles *Antigone*, Lucretius 3. 888–93. Heroes will even threaten this fate to their enemies: see, e.g., Achilles' cruel words to Hector at Homer *Iliad* 22.337–54.

152–3 The phrasing makes good use of chiasmus (**dilaceranda feris – alitibusque/praeda**), enjambement of **praeda** and the five-syllable word with which 152 ends. **praeda** is sardonic: after her help in the battle she deserved a share in the 'spoils' (see *OLD* s.v. 'praeda' 1) but instead *she* is the 'prey' (*OLD* s.v. 'praeda' 2) of wild beasts, who are the only ones to benefit now. Ovid's Ariadne (*Heroides* 10.83–7) even speculates on the precise animals which will feed on her body. The final words of line 153 allude to the fear that the spirit of an unburied corpse has no rest in the afterlife at least for a century (Virgil *Aeneid* 6.325–30) and also perhaps look forward to the sacrifice of another young woman (Polyxena) who is to be butchered at the tomb of Achilles (366–70). The passion of the words here is enhanced by the 't' alliteration.

154–7 Ariadne cannot believe that human beings could have given birth to such a monster as Theseus and speculates that it must have been a lioness (**leaena**) or else a stretch of treacherous water. This form of insult is found in Homer (*Iliad* 16.33–5), imitated by Virgil's Dido (*Aeneid* 4.365–7) and Ovid's Scylla (*Met*.8.120–1). Catullus created a whole poem (60) from the idea.

154 **solā** agrees with **rupe** with some transference of the epithet so that 'under a lonely crag' hints that the lioness is too cruel to socialise even with other lions. **genuit** is the perfect tense of *gigno* and **quaenam** is an indignant question form (as at 40.1).

155 The focus on the sea is not merely rhetorical, but is appropriate to her position on the shore. **conceptum ... exspuit** might suggest abortion or miscarriage as it implies rejection of the child. There is also effective alliteration and assonance of *sp*u̲mantibu*s* ex*sp*u̲it u̲ndi*s*.

156 Ariadne rattles off the three names **Syrtis ... Scylla ... Charybdis** in an impressive tricolon crescendo of **quae ... quae ... quae ...** The **Syrtis** are the treacherous shallows off the African coast; **Scylla** was loved by Poseidon and turned by her rival Amphitrite into a sea-monster who devoured sailors who sailed near her cave; **Charybdis** was the whirlpool off Sicily, a peril faced successfully by Jason and also by Odysseus (Homer *Odyssey* 12.234–60, 426–46). The descriptive epithets are well chosen: **rapax** (deriving from *rapio*) suggesting the 'snatching' of prey, while **vasta** connotes the all-engulfing desolate and monstrous mouth of Charybdis.

157 Ariadne juxtaposes all the positive words **dulci praemia vita** and does not need to spell out again what **talia** refers to.

158–9 Ariadne speculates on Theseus' motivation, suddenly according him more credit. The pluperfect tense of **fuerant** suggests that Theseus 'had never' entertained the idea of **conubia. cordi** *esse* + dative means 'to be dear to'. Ariadne had not met Theseus' father (Aegeus) but she imagines him in strikingly unpleasant terms, with strong 'p' alliteration to enhance the effect: he is **prisci** ('old school', 'traditional'), his 'orders' (**praecepta**) are **saeva** ('savage' (cf. 203) – like father, like son) and he inspired dread (**horrebas**). When we meet him later on (212–45), he is nothing like Ariadne's picture here.

160–1 Ariadne would even have enjoyed (**iucundo**) being his slave, with three words all denoting 'service': **famularer serva labore**. The phrase **quae famularer** is a relative purpose clause ('so that I could serve . . .').

162 This is a lovely line for an unlovely act, showing Ariadne even now romanticising her beloved. His feet are **candida** (denoting beauty as well as whiteness: cf. 86.1), and she can 'caress' them (**permulcens**). **vestigia** (usually meaning 'footsteps') here for the first time in Latin means 'feet' by metonymy, recalling the way her thread allowed him to retrace his footsteps in the Labyrinth (cf. *vestigia* used of Theseus' steps (113)). The sensuous pleasure of the foot massage is not just Ariadne's – the 'l' alliteration and the emphasis on 'water' in **liquidis . . . lymphis** seek to attract the recipient also. Ariadne is a skilled persuader, who tries to sell her charms to her absent lover.

A Level

163   purpurea veste is an ironic touch as the scene described is one
depicted on a purple coverlet (47–50) and so this character, depicted on
a purple coverlet, promises to give her lover a purple coverlet. This also
acts as a gentle reminder to the reader, who may have forgotten that
Ariadne herself is a depiction as it is some time since we heard about
the *vestis* itself. The line is a 'golden line' (see 129n.). There may also be
sexual significance in her mentioning the inviting bed she will spread
for him.

164–70   Ariadne pulls herself together and reminds herself (and us)
that she is, in fact, alone and unheard. She returns to the grim reality
after her four lines of deluded fantasy. It is also another ironic touch (as
at 169–70) as *we*, of course, can, in fact, hear her clearly, although we
cannot speak back to her.

164   Note the juxtaposition of **ignaris nequiquam**, which stresses the
futility of the speech: and cf. *nequiquam vanis* in 111.

165–6   externata shows Ariadne commenting on her own madness as
demonstrated by her behaviour. 'Talking to the winds' was a common
way to indicate 'wasting one's time' (cf. 142n.), but here the stock phrase
is used literally as she really is talking to the winds.

167–8   Ariadne speculates. By now (**prope iam**) he is in the middle of
the sea, whereas she has gone nowhere. **versatur** simply means 'he is'
but has the 'turning' overtones of *verso* and captures the sense of his
ship tossing in the waves. The (non-existent) **mortalis** is sandwiched in
the middle of **vacua ... in alga** and we see the gritty detail of **alga**
(seaweed, as at 60) rather than any romanticised sandy beach. **mortalis**
looks forward ironically to the god (Bacchus), who is going to arrive at
line 251 and whom the viewer can see on the coverlet, although Ariadne
cannot.

169–70   Ariadne endows fate (**fors**) with malice (**nimis insultans ...
saeva**) – when, in fact, it was Theseus who deserves these terms. There
is a wry joke in the play on **auris** ('breezes' 164) and **aures** ('ears' 170):
aures do not hear me, but only *aurae*. **nimis** shows that she

(understandably) feels that her suffering is unreasonably bad, as **fors** ('fortune') has 'even' (**etiam**) 'begrudged' (**invidit**) her the small consolation of an audience. This is again ironic as we are the audience which she claims not to have.

171 Ariadne, deprived of any human or meteorological audience, directs her words to the divine Jupiter. **omnipotens** suggests that since he can do everything, he can certainly do something to help her.

171-2 The counterfactual wish ('if only Athenian ships had never touched the harbour of Crete') is well known as the opening words of Euripides' *Medea*, imitated also by Ennius in the opening lines of his *Medea* (fr.253-4W). Ariadne wishes that they had never come 'in the first place' (**tempore primo**), which balances (in a chiasmus) her fate now 'in my final hour'(**extremo tempore**).

172-4 The juxtaposition of the place names makes 172 a 'golden line' (see 129n.). Even in her distress, Ariadne can still speak with a learned allusive style, using 'Cnossian' (for Cretan, whose capital was Cnossos) and 'Cecropian' (for Athenian, whose first ruler was the half-man, half-snake Cecrops). Even more striking is the string of understatements: **puppes** literally means 'poop decks' but here stands for the entire ships in synecdoche. If just the 'poop decks of Cecrops' had not even 'touched the shore' of Cnossos and the 'sailor' had not 'untied his ship's cable', then her fate would have been so different: her doom was sealed by this sequence of tiny actions.

173 The unpleasant adjectives go together at the front and the nouns at the end enclosing the central participle, while **indomito ... dira ... stipendia tauro** is in chiastic order. The 'taxes' (**stipendia**) were the 'chosen young men and glory of the unmarried girls' (78) which were sent to be eaten by the Minotaur. **religasset** is the shortened form of the pluperfect subjunctive *religavisset* (as is **requiesset** in 176).

174 For **perfidus**, cf. 133. **navita** is also a cutting jibe – Theseus is now nothing more than a sailor, and a treacherous one at that.

175–6 Theseus is now described as a **malus hospes**, and the word **crudelia** is tucked inside the phrase **dulci . . . forma** just as his cruelty was hidden within his attractive form. The word **hospes** is sardonic – he was invited in to 'rest' in their home, with the two key words **requiesset sedibus** juxtaposed. The enjambement of 175–6 also enacts Ariadne's outpouring of emotion.

177–87 Ariadne is alone and trapped, as are other characters in ancient literature such as Philoctetes (abandoned on the island of Lemnos by the treacherous Greeks, a fate similar to Ariadne's), Daedalus and Icarus on Crete who seek to escape from King Minos (Ariadne's father) by flying. This passage is striking for its repeated use of rhetorical questions and deliberative subjunctives, directed ostensibly at Jupiter.

177–82 **referam** and **petam** could be either future indicative or deliberative subjunctives: **speram** (180) and **consoler** (182) must be subjunctives and it makes sense to read all four verbs as deliberative ('am I to . . .?'), showing well her hesitant helplessness.

177 **referam** has the sense of 'turn back to', appropriate for one who has left her home and cannot return. **nitor** is an outraged present indicative: 'what hope am I relying on when I am **perdita?**'

178–9 Ida was a mountain in her native Crete: mentioning the name may perhaps indicate a pang of homesickness. Ariadne now begins to answer her own questions: 'making for mountains' is impossible when there is a massive sea (**gurgite lato**) between them and her.

179 **truculentum** ('angry' or 'ferocious') is a pathetic fallacy, as if the sea itself were hostile towards her (cf. 63.16), but its primary purpose is to stress the impossibility of crossing it: not just a large sea but a 'stormy' sea, here made epic in tone with the word **ponti** rather than *maris*. *pontus* is also a Greek word and it is apt that this Cretan girl uses her own language. Note here also the intensification of the idea of 'separation' with the two near-synonyms **discernens . . . dividit** and the adjective **lato**.

180–1 Ariadne's mother Pasiphae mated with a bull to produce the Minotaur, and it is interesting to speculate how much affection her father bore for the monster born of his wife's bestiality, a 'son' whom he locked in the labyrinth. Ariadne assumes that her family was hostile because of her fratricide, although (again) the Minotaur was at best half-brother and, in fact, a murderous monster (see 150n.). The theme of fratricide is picked up again (albeit very differently) at 399 in Catullus' moralising epilogue, where 'brothers soaking their hands in brothers' blood' is one of the dreadful aspects of modern society which explain the absence of gods from our lives. Her despair is well evoked in **sperem** – she cannot even 'hope' for his help. **respersum** agrees with **iuvenem** (referring to Theseus): he is not named, reflecting the way her father would view her actions as simply those of a girl following a young man. **quem** has the question suffix -**ne** attached to it, as does **quine** in 183, keeping the questioning tone of the sentence uppermost even in the relative clauses.

182 Ariadne's words are sardonic, completing the trio of comforts denied her – no home (**Idaeos . . . montes 178**), no father and now no husband with which she could console herself. **memet** (the -**met** suffix strengthens the pronoun **me**) is perhaps self-pitying and there is obvious sarcasm in her description of the 'faithful love' of this man who has deserted her.

183 Theseus is pulling at the oars as if 'bending' (**incurvans**) them. **lentos** means 'pliant' (i.e. not breaking under the pressure of the rower) but also has the sense of 'sluggish', suggesting Theseus' impatience with his own slow progress. Ariadne imagines that Theseus is rowing over the sort of **gurgite** which she has just (178) described as separating her from her homeland.

184–7 Ariadne's lonely despair finds its expression in two series of anaphoras: **nullo . . . nulla . . . nulla** and then **omnia . . . omnia . . . omnia**: the first one is a tricolon decrescendo as the three phrases diminish in length, the latter is a tricolon crescendo where the opposite occurs.

A
Level

184–5 Ariadne cannot stay but cannot leave: the transferred epithet **sola** (agreeing with **insula**) enhances her sense of isolation (see 177–87n.), and **pelagi** (like **ponti** at line 179, a Greek word for 'sea') is used for epic poetic effect. **cingentibus undis** is an ablative absolute with explanatory force: there is no way out 'since the waves are encircling' her.

186–7 The final syllable of the second **nulla** is scanned long by position before the double consonant which begins **spes**, as at 17.24. The silence (**muta**) around her has already been alluded to (and broken) in lines 164–6, but Ariadne's words are ironic in view of what will come. Far from being **muta**, Bacchus and his entourage make a terrific din (254–64), and the island is not **deserta** once the bacchants arrive, and (far from facing **letum**), Ariadne will marry a god and thus be immortal when Theseus is merely a dead hero.

188–91 Ariadne announces her intention to appeal to the gods and secure vengeance – a vengeance which (as it turns out) is simultaneously granted and rendered unnecessary in the lines to come. She will be saved by Bacchus and so not die, but Theseus has still done wrong and will be punished with the death of his own father (202–48), as ordained by Jupiter (204).

188–9 Ariadne imagines a lingering, weary death (**languescent ... fesso**), like falling asleep (cf. 5.5–6, Lucretius 3.466, Horace *Odes* 1.24.5). The words have a drowsy alliteration of 'l' and suitably heavy syllables in **languescent**, along with an interesting use of 'lights' for 'eyes' (as at 51.11–12), which is counter-intuitive in describing death but which enacts the process with the juxtaposition **lumina morte**. The second image (of senses 'withdrawing') reminds us of the contemporary poet Lucretius' theory that the *anima* links the senses together in what we would call the nervous system, whereby sleep is a temporary, and death a permanent, disconnection of the channels of sensation.

190 **ante** (line 188) is only translated when we meet **quam**. Ariadne is not expecting to see justice done in her lifetime – she merely promises to voice her demands before dying. The verbs **exposcam** and **comprecer**

A
Level

are both subjunctives, indicating a sense of purpose or expectancy (see AG § 551c). A *multa* was a financial penalty, and it is ironically understated in a highly rhetorical passage to use so pedestrian a word, especially in juxtaposition with the explanatory **prodita**.

191 This line completes the sentiment of line 190 in different words, adding the emotive phrase **postrema . . . hora** ('in my final hour') and softening the 'demand' (**exposcam**) into a 'prayer' (**comprecer**). Ariadne trusts in the **fidem** of the gods – and later events prove her right.

192 multantes picks up **multa**, and the three words **multantes vindice poena** add up to a devastating triad of punishment. She postpones naming the avenging agents until the next line, with their name (**Eumenides**) emphasised in enjambement.

193–4 The **Eumenides** were the 'Kindly Ones' or 'Erinyes' who punished murder – especially murder of kinsfolk as in Aeschylus' *Oresteia* – and perjury (Homer *Iliad* 19. 259–60, Hesiod *Works and Days* 803–4). Such beings are often depicted as having snakes entwined in their hair (e.g. Aeschylus *Choephoroi* 1049–50, Virgil *Georgics* 4.481–2, *Aeneid* 6.280–1, Horace *Odes* 2.13.35–6). The construction here is as follows: the subject of the verb **praeportat** is the **frons** which is described as **redimita** ('wreathed') with 'snaky hair'. **quibus** (in the dative of posession) refers to the Eumenides, and the sentence runs: 'Eumenides, whose forehead, wreathed with snaky hair, bears forth the blast of anger from their heart.' **exspirantes** here goes with **iras** and is intransitive (their 'blast of anger'). Line 194 uses snake-like sibilance as well as plosive 'p' alliteration.

195–7 Ariadne's emotion is emphasised by the repetition (**huc huc**), the raw grief of **vae misera** (cf. 8.15n.) and the impressive four-adjective catalogue **inops ardens amenti caeca** sandwiched by the basic phrase **cogor . . . furore**: note also the tricolon crescendo of: a) **inops** b) **ardens** c) **amenti caeca furore**.

196 The word *medulla* properly denotes the 'marrow' of the bones but comes to mean the 'innermost heart' here, as in 93, 35.15, 45.16, 58b.8.

A Level

197 The passive verb **cogor** is expressive: she is 'compelled' to do this by her **amenti furore** (literally: 'mindless madness') and she is 'blind' (**caeca**) and 'helpless' (**inops**) in her blazing passion (**ardens**). This is all by way of excusing what is now an aggressive act of cursing.

198 Ariadne may be blind with fury but her feelings are **verae. pectore ab imo** picks up and varies **extremis . . . medullis** in 196.

199 **vos,** addressing the Furies, is, of course, not necessary with the verb **nolite** but the phrase shows her making a peremptory command to them. **vanescere** is effective: the *-scere* suffix indicates 'becoming' (as in *senesco, calesco, irascor*) and so this verb means 'to grow *vanus*' and thus 'come to nothing'.

200–1 Ariadne prays that Theseus should suffer as she has suffered. 'Making the punishment fit the crime' is an element of other legends such as Tantalus whose impious cannibalistic feast is punished with his permanent hunger, or Arachne whose boast that she could spin as well as Minerva is punished with her being turned into a spider. The common element here is that Theseus abandoned Ariadne because he was *immemor* (135) and this same forgetfulness will be his undoing when used against his father. Just as he did not think of Ariadne, so he will not think of his father's injunction to change the sails on his ship and will cause the old man's death. The phrasing is correlative: 'with what sort of (**quali**) state of mind he left me ... with that (**tali**) state of mind let him ...'. Also notice here the sequence of heavy syllables and 'e' assonance in line 200 and the expressive verb **funestet** (derived from *funus*) in line 201 applied to **seque suosque** (with epic polysyndeton).

202–48 Catullus now explains how the curse is fulfilled when Theseus returns to Athens. This passage adds to the complexity of the *ecphrasis* in that it involves flashback to the farewell scene between Aegeus and Theseus and also flashforward to the dénouement of this storyline. It also adds to the moral complexity as Ariadne's quest for justice produces undeserved suffering for Aegeus, a character who is (like Ariadne) a

A Level

victim of Theseus, who is nothing like the grumpy old man whom Ariadne had imagined (159) and who is described in sympathetic terms as a loving father throughout this passage, sometimes even echoing Ariadne's own suffering (e.g. 219).

203 A neat symmetrical line: noun A – adjective B – verb – adjective A – noun B. **exposcens** picks up **exposcam** from line 190 while *saevus* has been used to describe the orders of Theseus' father (159) and fate itself (169). Ariadne herself is sad (**maesto pectore**) and afraid (**anxia**).

204 Ariadne earlier (191) mentioned the **caelestum ... fidem** and her trust is justified as the **caelestum ... rector** (Jupiter) nods assent here, and later on (251–64) Bacchus rescues her. **invicto numine** ('with unconquered power') is both ablative of description applied to Jupiter and also instrumental ablative, showing the means whereby he granted her wish (**annuit**). The word *numen* derives from the archaic word *nuo* ('I nod my head'), showing the divine ability to change the world simply by nodding assent, as in Homer (*Iliad* 1.528–30). Catullus' line is imitated at Virgil *Aeneid* 9.106.

205–6 The three spheres of earth, sea and sky all tremble, and the phrase makes good use of the tricolon crescendo, which climaxes with Jupiter's own sphere of the heavens. **horrida** is predicative of the ruffled surface of the sea after the nod, while the final phrase gives us a wonderful image of how the sky (**mundus**) shook the 'gleaming stars' (**micantia sidera**).

207–8 These lines use a range of metaphors: **consitus** is from *consero* ('I plant, sow') and gives the image of Theseus' mind like a field planted with 'murky darkness' – **mentem** being accusative of respect. *caligo* is properly 'darkness' but here denotes mental fog, which confuses and restricts intelligence and memory: philosophers often viewed truth as light and error as darkness (e.g. Plato *Republic* 508d, Lucretius 2.59–61). **caeca** ('blind') points out that the darkness renders us unable to see. **oblito dimisit pectore**: 'he let slip from his forgetful heart'.

209 The word **mandata** (repeated at 214 and 232) is key to understanding this passage as the fate of Aegeus rests on his son's ability to carry out 'orders'. The word also has the sense 'entrusted' (from *mando*), which refers back neatly to Ariadne who entrusted herself rashly to his care.

210 The juxtaposition of **dulcia . . . maesto** is deliberate, as the white sails would, indeed, have been 'sweet' to the 'sad' parent. The tale is here sketched in rough outline: the sails are referred to with the unspecific word **signa** ('signals' the exact word which Aegeus uses at 222), to be elaborated in greater detail at 233–7. **nec** is to be taken with both **sustollens** and **ostendit**.

211 Erectheus was the great-grandfather of Aegeus, and so **Erectheum** means 'Athenian' and the port referred to is the Piraeus. **sospitem** is in emphatic position at the start of the line telling Aegeus the vital fact ('safe') which any anxious parent would want to know above all else.

212–37 A flashback to events preceding the expedition and the emotional leave-taking of father and son.

212 **ferunt** ('they say') distances the author from his narrative (cf. **perhibent** 76, 124n.), while **olim** also shows that this is all part of the legend from long ago (cf. 2, 76, 124).

212–13 **classi** is ablative ('with his fleet') and is taken with **linquentem**. The **divae** referred to is the goddess Athena, patron goddess of Athens. The pathos is apparent: Theseus is 'leaving the protective walls of the goddess' as Aegeus is 'entrusting his son to the winds'.

214 The accusative participle **complexum** refers to Aegeus and the construction is indirect statement after **ferunt** ('they say that after embracing him he gave such instructions to the young man').

215–37 Aegeus' farewell, couched in two long sentences composed in difficult syntax and awkward structure, is suggestive perhaps of 'an old man's rambling way of speaking' (Quinn).

215-16 Aegeus addresses Theseus twice with the vocative **nate** ('son') in emphatic position at the start of the lines, adding the further poignant details that he is his only son (**unice**) and that he was 'restored' to him when he was 'on the very edge of old age' – a time of life when he was both in need of filial protection and unlikely to beget further children. Aegeus is forced to **dimittere** his son – who then **dimisit** his father's instructions (208). **longā** goes with **vitā** and is an ablative of comparison with **iucundior** ('sweeter than long life').

217 Theseus had spent much of his life in Troezen and his father Aegeus did not meet him until he had made the journey to Athens as a grown man: for the legends of his journey, see *OCD* s.v. 'Theseus'. **reddite** is the vocative of the perfect passive participle from *reddo*. **extrema . . . fine** is something of a tautology and serves to add emphasis to Aegeus' old age.

218-19 Aegeus has no choice (**eripit invito**) in what is caused by his **fortuna** and his son's quest for glory. There is apt juxtaposition of **mea ac tua** and then **mihi te**, both expressive of the father's closeness to his son, and **fervida** ('boiling' meaning here 'hot-headed' or 'impetuous') is often used of anger and passion (e.g. Virgil *Aeneid* 12.951). The phrase **fervida virtus** well conveys the mixture of courage and impetuous passion which makes up Theseus – like his father, whose own rash qualities will cause his unnecessary suicide when he jumps to conclusions (and to his death) in lines 243-5.

219 The sense of **languida** is that of eyes 'drooping' in sleep or death (as of Ariadne at 188).

220 The language is expressive: **saturata** is 'feasted full' (cf. *satur* at 21.9, 32.10) and Aegeus suggests the image of the banqueter satisfied after feasting – ironically, as the dreadful feast in prospect is one of human flesh to a Minotaur.

221 The old man uses the tautologous phrase **gaudens laetanti pectore** to emphasise his feelings here, framed by another protest of reluctance (**non ego te . . . mittam**).

222 Aegeus has no choice about Theseus' departure, but he seems to have control over the sails (**non sinam**). Using sails of 'favourable fortune' would perhaps be tempting fate.

223 The lamentation (**querellas**) is premature, even if justified in the event, and Aegeus ironically enacts the lament in announcing that he intends to do it: he perhaps hopes that by thus rehearsing funeral laments, his son may think twice about going. **mente** is ablative after **expromam** ('I will bring forth from my mind', cf. 65.3) and the phrase **mente querellas** has powerful assonance of 'e'.

224 Defiling the head with earth and dust is a gesture of grief, as performed by Achilles over the dead Patroclus (Homer *Iliad* 18. 23–5), Priam over his dead son Hector (Homer *Iliad* 24. 163–5) and later Evander over his dead son Pallas (Virgil *Aeneid* 10.844). Aegeus is described as behaving like an epic king to add grandeur to his very personal emotion. We are reminded of his old age with **canitiem**.

225 There is elegant balancing of adjectives and nouns around a central verb, with **infecta** (from *inficio*) agreeing with **lintea** and **vago** with **malo**.

226 Note the rhetorical repetition of **nostros . . . nostrae** at the start of each of the two halves of the line, and also the characterisation of Aegeus' feelings, first as **luctus** and then with the more expressive **incendia mentis**, expressive of the old man's fiery heart.

227 The sailcloth (**carbasus**), which is 'darkened with Iberian rust' is to 'indicate' (**dīcet** is the present subjunctive from *dīcare* in a final clause) Aegeus' grief. *ferrugo Hibera* is a dark-purple colour (cf. Virgil *Aeneid* 6.303), and the geographical term **Hibera** adds to the anxiety of the old man seeing his son sail afar off: Spain was regarded as the far West.

228 The 'dweller on holy Itonus' refers to the goddess Athena: Itonus was a town in Thessaly with a famous sanctuary of the goddess. The phrase is fully in keeping with the formal urgency of the prayer that he uses the sort of terms which we find in such oaths and prayers, and he continues the high style with **sedes ... Erechthei** and **facito ut**, cf. 61.1–2, 36. 11–17. The wording of the prayer is important if it is to be heard.

229–30 For Erechtheus see 211n. The lines have a pleasing balance, whereby **genus ac sedes** are central and the enjambement throws emphasis onto **annuit**. The juxtaposition of **sanguine dextram** indicates vividly the blood on the hands. For **annuit**, cf. 204n.

230 The Minotaur here is simply a bull (**tauri**) rather than the **monstrum** he was at 101 – or the brother he was to Ariadne at 181 – perhaps to make the prayer more achievable in the eyes of the goddess and to suggest that Aegeus is reassuring himself that his son could well perform the deed.

231 The formality of the prayer continues with the archaic future imperative **facito** (cf. 50.21) followed by **ut** + subjunctive ('see to it that ...'), the slightly pompous phrasing bringing out the regal character of the speaker and the divine audience addressed. **memor** and its opposite *immemor* are the terms by which Theseus is constantly found wanting, cf. 58, 248.

231–2 The metaphors are mixed. The instructions are to be **condita** ('stored' like treasure) and to 'thrive' like plants (**vigeant**, cf. 72 for this metaphor) in Theseus' heart and no passage of time (**aetas**) is to 'efface' (**oblitteret**) them as if they were an inscription blurred by time and the elements.

233 lumina (as at 188 and 51.12) means 'eyes' and **invisent** recalls **visere** in 211 to underline how Theseus failed to remember what was said. **colles** ('hills') would be the first things to be visible from out at sea and the word suggests that Theseus is to act before there is any chance of Aegeus himself seeing his ship, the urgency emphasised by **simul ac** ('as soon as'). The poet skilfully lets Aegeus' words prefigure exactly what will happen.

A
Level

234   The line is framed by the 'cloth of death' (**funestam . . . vestem**) and the sails are so described both because they (falsely) announce the death of Theseus and also because they (truly) bring about the death of Aegeus, as shown in the use of the same word at 246.

234-5   There is a neat contrast and parallelism in these lines, as **funestam** is placed at the beginning of one line, **candida** at the beginning of the other, and likewise the two antonymic verbs (**deponant: sustollant**) are placed midway in their respective lines. **undique** adds emphasis – do not leave such sails flying *anywhere*. The ropes (**rudentes**) are 'twisted' (**intorti**) because they are made from plaited threads and rushes.

236   The old man is impatient for good news, as **quam primum** brings out. The words **laetā gaudia** are juxtaposed to stress the joy he hopes for.

237   Aegeus says he will recognise him (**agnoscam**) when the 'successful time' will set him (**sistet**) on dry land. **aetas prospera** suggests Theseus' successful survival: **aetas** can mean 'time' and also 'life' and 'youth' and the three ideas come together to give a picture of the young survivor. Aegeus anticipates the sort of rapturous father-and-son reunion which we find in (e.g.) Homer *Odyssey* 16.172–221, 24.226–355.

238-40   The sentence is complex, with **haec mandata** both the subject of **liquere** and the object of **tenentem** which agrees with **Thesea**. The sentence then means: 'these orders, although Theseus held on to them previously with a fixed purpose, left him, just like clouds, beaten by the blast of the winds, leave the airy summit of a snowy mountain'. **liquere** is in the perfect tense in two senses here: the word is a simple perfect tense ('the orders "left" Theseus') and is also a 'gnomic' perfect in the simile describing how clouds 'leave' the mountain top: for this gnomic use, cf. 148 and 62.42n. **pulsae** is the past participle of *pello*.

239-40   An epic simile, based on Homer *Iliad* 5. 522–6, with the added touch of the words blown away by the winds which we find in 59, 164–5, and especially 142 (where see note). The vividness is enhanced by the powerful terms indicating height: the snow (**nivei**) on the peak and the high winds blowing there (**aereum**).

241 The father gazes from a high vantage point to look out for Theseus' ship sailing towards him, just as in similar fashion Ariadne sought a high vantage point from which to gaze at Theseus sailing away from her (126–7). Here Aegeus' desperation is brought out as he 'sought' (**petebat**) a view (**prospectum**) from the 'very top' (**summa**) of the citadel.

242 A 'golden' line (see 129n.) with abundant 'a' assonance expressing grief. The pathos of the old man 'wearing out' (**absumens**) his anxious eyes simply by weeping is also striking and used again at 68.55.

243 **cum primum** picks up **quam primum** from 236 and is consistent with Aegeus' impulsive nature. **infecti** (from *inficio*: cf. 225) shows the dark colour of the sails and – as the thing which Aegeus most dreaded – is placed straight after **cum primum** to show this. **lintea veli** is something of a tautology ('fabrics of the sail') but here brings out the extent to which the bad news covered the whole canvas.

244 Aegeus threw himself 'head first' (**praecipitem**), showing that his act was a deliberate act of suicide: notice how the poet brings out the height of his fall with the terms **scopulorum e vertice**, making a dreadful act even more dreadful.

245 **immiti fato** refers to the imagined grisly death inflicted by the Minotaur. The phrase is in the ablative with **amissum** ('taken away by a cruel fate').

246–50 Catullus ends this part of the *ecphrasis* with verbal echoes recalling the beginning of the episode: central themes are run through quickly once again, unravelling the story much as Theseus unravelled the thread in the labyrinth. **funesta ... paterna morte** refers to the latest incident described (i.e. the death of Aegeus); **ferox** reminds us of the killing of the Minotaur (73–4, 105–11), suggested also by the term **Minoidi** ('daughter of Minos') to describe Ariadne. Finally, we see the

A Level

picture with which the scene began (52ff.) of Ariadne gazing sadly on the seashore. **qualem . . . talem** reminds us of Ariadne's curse **quali . . . tali** (200-201), and the sentence ends with an appropriately maritime metaphor for Ariadne 'rolling many-layered cares inside her heart', recalling the earlier description of her in lines 52–4. Individual words add to this ring-composition effect: **immemori** in 248 looks back to *immemor* in 58, **prospectans** in 249 picks up *prospectans* in 52, **cedentem** (249) recalls 53, and **maesta** (249) picks up *maestis* in 60.

246-7   Theseus entered (**ingressus**) the **funesta tecta** of the **domūs**; the house is **funesta** by virtue of the **paterna morte** – and **morte** is emphasised with enjambement.

247-8   **qualem. . . talem** are correlatives ('the kind of **luctum** which he had inflicted . . . that sort he himself received') and hammer home the point of 'just deserts'. The **luctum** for Ariadne is both the heartbreak of being abandoned by her lover and also the bereavement caused by the death of her half-brother the Minotaur (150). **mente immemori** brings out the consistent selfishness of Theseus, who failed to think of Aegeus, just as he had failed to think of Ariadne, and **obtulerat** (from *offero*) declares agency rather than simply a sin of omission – he had actually 'presented' this grief to her.

249   This line is heavily spondaic, showing the motionless girl gazing out sadly at the 'keel' (**carinam**: used in synecdoche for the ship as a whole).

250   The rhythm picks up here with two dactyls to start this line showing the moving waves of care, as Ariadne is now actively 'turning' or 'rolling' her complex feelings in her heart. **saucia** shows her being 'wounded' both emotionally by love (as Dido at Virgil *Aeneid* 4.1, Phaedra at Euripides *Hippolytus* 392) and also by the physical plight she is left in where her life is in danger. **multiplices** well brings out the mixture of love, fear and anger which rage inside her.

251-64   While Ariadne is gazing out to sea, the god Dionysus/Bacchus is behind her, approaching with his retinue, to save her – an example of dramatic irony, whereby we know more than Ariadne, and also a reversal of fortune for the hitherto hapless girl.

251   parte ex alia reminds us that the poet is describing a picture on a coverlet and invites us to imagine the god as depicted 'elsewhere' on the tapestry. **Iacchus** is another name for the Greek god Dionysus, often called Bacchus or Liber in Latin. This mysterious god was himself the child of Zeus/Jupiter and a mortal woman Semele: she died when the god revealed himself fully to her, at which point Jupiter extracted the divine baby from her womb and implanted it in his thigh. The child was brought up by the nymphs of Mount Nysa (see 252n.) and the worship of this god was carried out especially by women (Maenads, **Thyades** (cf. 254), Bacchants) who would take to the mountains and there practise forms of ecstatic religious rites involving the killing and eating of wild animals. Dionysiac worship is examined in Euripides' tragedy *Bacchae*, a play which may be the source for some of Catullus' phrases here.

   florens volitabat is a striking pair of words: the speed shown in his 'flying' and his youthful energy in **florens** – literally, 'flowering'.

252   The line is mannered in the extreme to show the Greek sources of the imagery. **Nysigenis** ('born on Nysa') is a compound adjective of Greek formation while *thiasus* is a transliteration of a Greek noun meaning the 'company' of Dionysiac worshippers, used also of the frenzied band of Cybele's worshippers at 63.28. The Satyrs and Sileni are also Greek terms for the grotesque male attendants of the god – the young Satyrs were goat-like creatures in a permanent state of sexual arousal, while the old Sileni were usually drunk and always disorderly. Mount Nysa was traditionally seen as the source of the Dionysiac cult, although opinions differ as to its geographical location. Metrically the line is awkward, evoking the riotous crowd: the fifth foot is a spondee (cf. also 255, 258) and the final three feet are formed by two long words. The fifth-foot spondee was a feature of the Greek Callimachus and the Roman 'New Poets' and was satirised by Cicero (*ad Atticum* 7.2.1): Catullus uses it thirty times in this poem.

A Level

253 Catullus addresses a character directly in apostrophe (cf. 22–30, 69), emphasising the personal address with the vocative name and the repetition of **te . . . tuoque**. This sort of emotional direct address to a character in an epic poem goes back to Homer (e.g. *Iliad.* 16.584, *Odyssey* 14.54). **tuo amore** here means primarily 'his love for you' but there may also be a suggestion that Ariadne's subjective passion (for Theseus) makes her more attractive to the god.

253–4 The manuscript reading for 254 (*qui tum alacres*) is awkward: it appears to pick up the masculine singular subject of **incensus** but turns out to refer to the many female worshippers who 'raved' (**furebant**). This anomaly has led editors to suppose a lacuna between these lines. I have printed the emendation of Trappes-Lomax which removes any need for a lacuna and makes eminent sense.

254–5 The phrase **passim lymphata mente furebant** emphasises the madness and frenzy of the maenads (**Thyades**: on whom see 251n.), as does the repeated ritual cry **euhoe** (pronounced as two long syllables as at Horace *Odes* 2.19.7) which is not part of the syntax of the sentence. *lymphatus* derives from *lympha* ('water' or 'water-nymph') and means 'driven mad by the nymphs', adding a further supernatural level to the raving. **capita inflectentes** ('tossing their heads') refers to the familiar image of the maenads 'in ecstasy flinging back their head in the dewy air' (Euripides' *Bacchae* 864–5). Notice again the fifth-foot spondee and the single long word covering both the final feet (cf. 252n.).

256–9 The poet depicts the four groups of maenads doing different things with **pars . . . pars . . . pars . . . pars . . .** There is a fascinating sequence here of the harmless (playing percussion instruments), the savage (dismembered animals being thrown about) and the weird (wearing snakes).

256 The *thyrsus* was a staff tipped with vine-leaves or ivy (**tecta cuspide** is an ablative of description: 'with covered tip'). The brandishing of the *thyrsus* is another image of frenzied movement.

A Level

257 Another familiar aspect of Dionysiac ritual was the *sparagmos* or 'tearing to pieces' of an animal: the most notorious *sparagmos* was that in which the female relatives of King Pentheus tore him apart, thinking that he was a lion, as Dionysus' punishment for Pentheus' spurning of his rites in Thebes (see Euripides' *Bacchae* and Ovid *Metamorphoses* 3.511–733). The deliberate postponement of the noun **iuvenco** here may lead the reader to wonder exactly what, or who, is being dismembered. This line is heavily spondaic – which is surprising as it describes rapid movement – and perhaps suggests the trance-like state of the women.

258 Maenads could allegedly take venomous snakes into their hands without suffering harm, even being able (as here) to 'bind their speckled hide-garments with snakes which licked their cheeks' (Euripides' *Bacchae* 697–8). The poet makes onomatopoeic use of sibilant sounds to depict the snakes. **tortis** is the perfect passive participle of *torqueo* and has here the sense of 'writhing' or 'coiled'.

259 **orgia** usually denotes the 'rites' themselves but here refers to the secret mystical (**obscura**) cult objects contained in the wicker baskets (**cistis**). **celebrabant** has the sense of 'crowding around' as well as 'celebrating a festival' (cf. 302).

260 **orgia** is repeated in emphatic epanalepsis (cf. 132–3) and the meaning is 'rites' rather than the 'cult objects' of 259. **audire** ('to hear') has the sense of 'learn about', which is fitting for these secret objects, but there may be a touch of wry humour in that the poet is going on (261–4) to describe the loud music being produced by the Maenads. The **profani** are the uninitiated who are denied access to the cult and who 'long in vain' to find out about it. Several religious movements in the ancient world practised secrecy and initiation: see *OCD* s.v. 'mysteries'.

261–4 The sounds are evoked in expressive detail – although, of course, sounds cannot be portrayed in two-dimensional art such as the coverlet which Catullus purports to be describing. The sound effects include the hard 'p' alliteration of the drumbeat in **p**langebant ...

*p*roceris tym*p*ana *p*almis, the 't' alliteration and 'i' assonance of the cymbals in *tereti tenuis tinnitus*, the 'o' assonance of the bass notes of **raucisonos ... cornua bombos** and the shrieking 'i' assonance of **horribili stridebat tibia**.

261   The *tympanum* was more like a modern tambourine than a drum, consisting of hide stretched over one side of a wooden hoop. **proceris ... palmis** ('with outstretched palms') indicates that the drum was being beaten with the flat of the hand rather than a tight fist.

262   They 'produced faint ringing sounds on the rounded bronze' of the cymbal, such as we also find in the worship of Cybele (Propertius 3.17.36). These instruments (called *krotala* in Greek) were often associated with religious worship: see Euripides *Helen* 1308, Lucretius 2.618–20.

263–4   From percussion to wind instruments: the horn produces the low booming *bombus*, while the **tibia** (a reed instrument) emits a more blaring high-pitched sound, well evoked by the adjective **horribili**, the verb **stridebat** (a screeching sound) and the 'i' assonance of the two together. **multis** is a dative of reference (literally, 'in the case of many women, the horns . . .'). The **tibia** is foreign (**barbara**) as it is said to have originated in Phrygia (cf. 63.22) but it is possible that the term also alludes to the mode of the music being played. This is a magnificent 'golden line' with which to end the *ecphrasis* on the coverlet.

Poem 70

A poem of self-doubt, like 109 and unlike the confident happiness of (e.g.) poems 5, 7 and 107. 'Is this too good to be true? My woman says she wants me more than anybody else: but can I believe her?'

The poem is reminiscent of Callimachus *Epigram* 25:

> Callignotus swore to Ionis that he would never have anyone, male or female, more beloved than her. So, he swore; but they say truly that the oaths of lovers do not enter the ears of the gods. He is now ablaze with passion for a man, and there is no mention or reckoning of the wretched young woman, as of the Megarians.

The difference is one of focus: Callimachus is mocking the fickle Callignotus (as Catullus elsewhere mocks others, e.g. 23), whereas Catullus in this poem is doubting his own relationship. The final proverbial sentiment that a lover's words are to be written on the wind and water perhaps recalls Sophocles (fragment 741) and Plato (*Phaedrus* 276c) and is echoed by later poets (e.g. Propertius 2.28.8).

Metre: elegiac couplets (as are all the poems from 65 to 116).

1–2 The opening word is the emphatic **nulli** (dative of *nullus*, meaning the same as *nemini*) and the line is an indirect statement: 'my woman says (**dicit**) that she prefers to marry (**se nubere malle**) nobody ...'. **quam mihi** picks up the implied comparative in **nulli ... malle**: 'nobody else rather than me', and the generalised statement is elevated with the hyperbolic introduction of Jupiter himself as at 72.2. Jupiter was famous for his encounters with mortal women such as Semele and Alcmene, although none of these involved marriage. There is ambiguity in the opening lines: does the woman mean that she would rather marry Catullus than anybody else – or that she would rather remain single than marry him? The poet uses the general term **mulier** (rather than naming the 'woman') in order to lead nicely into the gender-generalisation of lines 3–4.

AS

3 The poet repeats **dicit** in a strongly emphatic position, throwing doubt on her words by stressing that they are just words, and 'my woman' (**mulier mea**) is now generalised into 'a woman' in asserting that women are faithless.

4 This misogynistic statement is intensified by **rapida** (the derivation from *rapio* suggests 'snatching' as well as 'rapid', having the destructive force of flood or hurricane) and also **cupido** (suggesting that the lover will believe anything she says when he is passionate). What is perhaps surprising is the gender of the speaker: elsewhere in love poetry, it is the ardent male who makes empty promises to his beloved to secure what he wants (as Theseus did to Ariadne at 64.139–48), whereas, here, the poet is the ardent one who is being duped by the girl's words. Catullus, as often, foils our expectations and reverses gender roles.

Poem 76

The poem argues that this love is an unjust misfortune which the poet prays to be rid of. He claims to have lived a good life and requests that the gods reward him for his good behaviour and release him from his suffering. The poem is structured partly as an interior dialogue, in which the poet addresses 'Catullus' (cf. 8.1, 52) and seeks to persuade himself to change his behaviour (even if he cannot alter his feelings), and partly as a prayer to the gods.

The poem is cleverly composed. The poet asks to be 'cured' of love, as his past good behaviour deserves this cure: but the examples of his past goodness are unrelated to his behaviour in the relationship and merely assert that he has neither deceived his fellow human beings (lines 3–4) nor abused the gods. Does this negative (**nec ... nec ... nullo**) boast qualify him for salvation? Should he not have done these things anyway? Later on, he says that he has done and said all the good things which anybody can do and say (lines 7–8) and the following line suggests that this goodness has all been bestowed on a thankless lover: but his manner of speaking in these lines is bland and vague (**quaecumque**

homines is highly unspecific) and presents a picture of the speaker as one who is struggling to find words to *justify* his feelings, although he is well able to find striking words (e.g. **excrucies** in the next line) to *describe* them.

The gods are a major part of this poem, both when referred to (4, 12) and when invoked: in prayer style he reminds them of his devotion to them (lines 3–4) to plead that *they* should now help *him*. He assumes the gods' opinion in **dis invitis** (line 12), arguing (presumably) that if the gods favour something it tends to go well, and so (as this relationship is not going well) the gods cannot favour it. Lines 17–26 continue this theme with a reminder to the gods that they help other people (and so should help him, too). The presence of the gods appears to hold the poem together, explaining the examples of piety at the beginning by looking forward to the prayer at the end. There is admittedly something of a contradiction between the helpless sickness of the poet in lines 19–26 and his self-addressed determination in lines 11–16, where the poet declares that he must 'win this battle' even if it is not possible. If, after all, he can do it by himself, then he does not need the gods: and if the gods will do it for him, then he need not do anything for himself. However, the history of divine help in cases of physical illness helps to endorse the poet's description of love as a sickness and also gains him the moral high ground of the *pietas* which frames the poem (2–4, 26).

This poem can be read as ironic – words presented 'in character' and with elements of mockery and sardonic humour. His words to himself (10–16) are (like poem 8) so much rhetoric expended in an attempt to persuade himself. His quasi-medical account of his 'sickness' in lines 20–2 is (like 51.5–12) another means of grasping the condition and thereby controlling it. His moral posturing at the beginning uses the language of social life (**fidem ... foedere**) to bolster up the collapsed dignity of a failed lover. The final four lines reveal the situation in a nutshell: after all the rhetoric, the medical language and the pious prayers, we are left with a man in love with a woman who does not love him and who does not care. The language of lines 23–5 is direct and simple after the prayers and the pleading. The final line then goes back

AS

to the 'moral' picture of the poet praying for justice, just as the final line of poem 8 reasserts the poet's resolve after the previous five lines have seen his hardness exposed as a sham. At the end of this poem, there is no confidence in religious faith and no cosy sense that the poet somehow emerges as morally victorious. We are left on this reading with an ironic text which shows us an attempt to offset the humiliation of rejection with the posturing of rectitude and piety: the literary quality of the poem allows us to see behind the rhetoric and the religiosity to the ineluctable sadness which all these words can do nothing to assuage.

1–2   homini is a possessive dative with **voluptas/est**. The present participle **recordanti** goes with **homini** and the **benefacta priora** are the object of the participle, so that the whole phrase means: 'if a man has any pleasure when he is recalling past good deeds'. **se cogitat esse pium** means 'he reflects that he is a dutiful man' rather than 'he thinks that he is dutiful' and the infinitives in lines 3–4 are likewise dependent on **cogitat**. The opening line is bleak: the only **voluptas** left to this person (of indeterminate gender) is recalling past good deeds, and this **voluptas** may not even exist (**si qua**). *pietas* is a tricky concept to define, connoting dutiful behaviour towards the state, the gods and other people: the poet helps us here with concrete examples in the following two lines.

3–4   The double negative (**nec . . . nullo**) reinforces the poet's feelings, shown also in the 'f' alliteration. The **benefacta** he recalls amount to a list of bad deeds he has *not* done rather than to positive contributions to human happiness: he later asks the gods for healing from the sickness which is love, and the implication is that he has done nothing bad to deserve such suffering. The misdeeds mentioned involve making oaths to deceive others, with **divum** and **homines** framing line 4. Understand **esse** with **abusum** to form the perfect infinitive of *abutor*. **divum** is the shortened form of the genitive plural *divorum* as at 64.134. The language is that of fidelity and honesty in agreements: a *foedus* is a formal agreement between men, while *fides* denotes 'trustworthiness'. This language is also used of the poet's relationship with Lesbia (cf. 87.3–4, 109.6) but the amatory application is not mentioned here until line 6.

5–6   **multa** goes with **gaudia** in the next line. The poet addresses himself in the vocative, as he did at 8.1 (cf. also 6.1, 7.10, 11.1), and the self-address is reinforced with **tibi** in the final place in the next line. The juxtaposition of **ingrato gaudia amore** brings out the ironic paradox that this 'thankless' love contains the possibility of 'joys' of a sort.

7–8   The **benefacta** of line 1 are broadened as 'whatever good things men can do or say to anyone' and the mournful tone of the repetitions here (**dicere . . . facere . . . dictaque factaque**) is striking.

9   The words **ingratae perierunt credita** suggest a financial metaphor (cf. 5.11n.), with the poet making a bad investment (as a creditor of emotion which has been invested in a heart which will not return it), with **ingratae** picking up **ingrato** from line 6. **menti** more often means 'mind' rather than 'heart' and the poet is perhaps suggesting that Lesbia was deliberately calculating in her behaviour rather than giving the emotional response he expected.

10   The string of monosyllables (**iam te cur**) in the rhetorical question perhaps evokes the poet's impatience with himself. **excrucies** is a strong word ('torture') and one which he uses again in a similar context at 85.2: the deliberative present subjunctive is effective with **amplius** and shows us the poet asking himself, 'why should you torment yourself any more?'

11   Toughening up the heart is something which the poet told himself to do in poem 8. **offirmas** here is intransitive ('toughen up') and **animo** is a local ablative ('in your heart'). There is a spatial metaphor in **istinc te ipse reducis** of 'bringing yourself back from that place' in the sense of 'come back to your senses'. I have printed Ellis' conjecture **te ipse** instead of the standard text *teque* (whose redundant *-que* makes it almost certain to be wrong).

AS

12   **dis** is the contracted form of *deis*. **dis invitis** is an ablative absolute construction: 'as the gods are against this' and builds on the protestations of his religious good behaviour in lines 2–4: the gods would not want so virtuous a citizen to suffer like this. The word **miser** is well placed at the end of the line and the sentence and acts as a summary of the forlorn state he is in (cf. 19, 8.1, 51.5, 64.57, 64.71).

13–14   The answer to the question of lines 11–12 (**quin tu . . . miser?**) comes at once with the repeated emphasis of **difficile est** and the juxtaposition of **longum subito**: ending a short relationship suddenly might be easy, but not a lengthy one. The phrase seems to have been something of a proverbial truism and is found in the fragments of the Greek comic poet Menander (Frag. 726).

14   **verum** is a strong adversative particle ('and yet') and **efficias** is a jussive present subjunctive ('you must manage this'), as is **facias** in 16. **qua lubet** (literally, 'in whatever way it pleases') means 'somehow or other' as at 40.6.

14–16   The anaphora of **hoc . . . haec . . . hoc . . . hoc** builds up the emphasis. The poet's salvation is painted in almost military terms as a means of securing safety (**salus**) and a battle which must be won (expressed in the heavily spondaic word **pervincendum**). **pote** means 'possible' (see 17.24 and cf. **potis** at line 24) and the final statement amounts to the paradox that he must do something even if it is not possible. The poet's wrestling with his need to achieve something which (he feels) is beyond him is well expressed in the starkest terms.

17   **vestrum est** means 'it is your role' (see *OLD* s.v. 'vester' 1d). Gods in the ancient world were not always renowned for their sympathy for mortals and some (such as the Epicureans) regarded the gods' 'blessed' state as requiring a degree of detachment from our concerns. On the other hand, we have the evidence of the dedications vowed and made because of survival both from sickness and calamity: temples have objects and tablets which were vowed to them in the event of successful outcomes, especially when they involved recovery from sickness.

Juvenal even tells us (10.349–50) that the gods will give us everything which is most appropriate for us as man is 'dearer to the gods than he is to himself'. **si quibus** is the dative plural of *si quis* ('if . . . to anybody').

18 **extremam . . . opem** frames the line and the dreadful situation of death is intensified with **ipsa**. The argument here is *a fortiori*: you have helped people when they are dying [when they need a huge amount of help], so you can certainly help me now with this sickness.

19-20 Catullus calls on the gods with formal imperatives (**aspicite . . . eripite**) rather than the more colloquial jussive subjunctives he uses to himself. **puriter** sounds oddly sanctimonious and is a sign of the poet's struggling to find the words he needs to express his pain. His anguish (of unrequited love) is called a disease (**pestem**) and a disaster (**perniciem**) and the two alliterative nouns amount to a hendiadys ('ruinous plague'), just as earlier on (10) he said that he was 'torturing' himself. The concept of love as a disease has a long history and Propertius (1.1.26–7) later continues the idea of love needing medical attention.

21-2 The medical language of **pestem** in 20 is expanded into a medical history of depression: compare and contrast the very physical symptoms of love which the poet listed in poem 51.

23-6 The poet continues to explain his needs: he is not asking for his feelings to be reciprocated, nor for her to become faithful, but is simply seeking freedom from disease.

23 **non iam** is heartfelt: after all he has suffered, he is 'no longer' asking for love. **illud** is explained in the clause **contra . . . illa**, 'I am not asking for that any longer, (namely) for her to love me in return': **contra** here is adverbial ('in return') rather than a preposition.

24 **potis** means the same as **pote** in line 16 – 'possible'. **pudica** derives from *pudeo* and has the sense of 'acknowledging the power of shame' or 'being sexually respectable' (cf. 15.5, 16.4, 21.12, in all of which it relates to public shame). For Lesbia's alleged promiscuity, cf. 11.17–20.

25   The language of sickness returns with love described as **hunc morbum** and the poet's aim as **valere**.

26   The ring composition is a powerful closural device: the poem ends as it began with *pietas*.

Poem 85

The shortest poem by Catullus. What seems to be an emotional *cri de coeur* is couched in a compact and starkly expressed couplet, asserting that love and hate easily coexist and are, in fact, two sides of the same coin, the opposite of both being indifference. This theme is explored further in poems 72, 75, 76, 83, 92.

   There is great artistry in this tiny poem: the opening phrase (**odi et amo**) is metrically identical to the final word (**excrucior**) and there is a neat contrast of active and passive in **faciam ... fieri**: the imaginary 'you' asking 'why I do that' in line 1 assumes that the poet has a choice in the matter and is actively directing his feelings, whereas the poet's answer in line 2 states that he is the passive victim of feelings beyond his control.

1   The statement of two apparently incompatible feelings demands clarification. The alliteration of 'f' is harsh and adds to the mood of dissonance in the poet's heart.

2   The four verbs in this line all denote the poet's passive plight: he lacks knowledge (**nescio**) but feels it is being done to him (**fieri sentio**) and it is torture (**excrucior**: for this verb, cf. 76.10).

Poem 88

The first in a sequence of four poems attacking a certain Gellius, who is commonly identified as L. Gellius Poplicola: a man who was said to have slept with his stepmother Palla and who may even have been one of the 'three hundred lovers' enjoyed by Lesbia according to poem 11.18. There is also evidence that he was involved in the prosecution of Caelius in 56 BC. He tried and failed to kill Brutus and Cassius after their assassination of Julius Caesar in 44 BC, becoming a consul in 36 BC and fighting on the (losing) side of Antony in the battle of Actium in 31 BC. For more on Gellius and his complex family tree, see Wiseman, *Cinna the Poet*, pp. 119–29.

Catullus attacks him for seducing his uncle's wife and her daughter (poems 74, 88, 89, 90), for giving oral sex to men (80) and for seducing the poet's own beloved (91). The very last poem in the collection (116) announces the poet's intention to attack Gellius – presumably with the poems which appear earlier in the collection. What is striking about this poem is that it succeeds in being extremely rude without using primary obscenities: Catullus gains his effects with innuendo and allusion rather than simple crudity.

The structure of the poem is simple: the first half (1–4) is a series of questions addressed to the court of public morals: the second half (5–8) is the verdict delivered. The whole poem is a neat exercise in ring composition (A–B–C–C–B–A) thus:

1–2 sexual behaviour
3 family members
4 quantum suscipiat?
5 suscipit . . . quantum
6 family members
7–8 sexual behaviour

1 Catullus addresses Gellius with a vocative, as if he were facing prosecution, but the **is** pronoun (and the allegations atached to it) describe 'someone' (third person) committing the acts of which Gellius is guilty: misbehaviour with his 'mother' (it may have been, in fact, his stepmother Palla, wife of his father Lucius Gellius). Palla was also married to Marcus Valerius Messala, who already had a daughter Valeria, who may be the 'sister' referred to here. The poet is not concerned to report facts fairly, but rather to make a powerful case.

2   prurit means essentially 'itches' but here has the sense of 'gets the urge' as at 16.9. **pervigilat** simply means 'stays awake all night', with the innuendo that his nocturnal activities last all night, their sexual nature indicated with the ablative absolute describing the clothing thrown off. The poet dwells on the nakedness and the sexual stamina with scandalised prurience.

3   Gellius had (according to poem 74) silenced his censorious uncle by cuckolding him and so 'does not allow him to be a husband' as his place has been usurped.

4   ecquid is an interrogative particle meaning here: 'is it not the case that…?' or simply 'surely' (see *OLD* s.v. 'ecquid' 1b). **sceleris** is a partitive genitive with **quantum** (literally, 'how much of wickedness') and **suscipiat** is in the subjunctive as this is an indirect question.

5   suscipit picks up **suscipiat** from the previous line in a manner reminiscent of the lawcourts, and the vocative exclamation **o** shows a raising of the heat (cf. 24.1, 28.9, 33.1) as this judge thunders his verdict. The poet now uses the imagery of crime as filth needing to be washed away with hyperbolic examples drawn from mythology to show the extent of Gellius' unwashable filth. **Tethys** was the wife of **Oceanus** (the river which flowed around the edges of the world) and she is called **ultima** as she lived on the furthest borders of the world (cf. 11.11–12). **nympharum** here refers to the Oceanids, who were the daughters of Oceanus and Tethys (see *OCD* s.v. 'Oceanus (mythological)'). The imagery here is high-flown to prepare for the bathetic conclusion in the following couplet, but what makes this mythological example especially apt is that Oceanus and Tethys were brother and sister and so this incestuous pair of water-beings are named as incapable of cleaning the incestuous Gellius.

7   The poem works to its climactic conclusion with lengthy phrasing (**nihil est quicquam sceleris**, which combines *nec est quicquam* and *nihil est* into an unnecessary tautology) and a spatial metaphor for further crime: **quo prodeat ultra** literally means 'to where he could advance further' – i.e. he could not make any further progress in his scandalous career.

8   The final line is a wonderful cartoon-like image of Gellius 'lowering his head and swallowing himself'. The verb **voret** has been similarly used of Gellius' oral sex in 80.6. The sense of the final line is that this man has seduced everyone else, legal and illegal, and now might as well seduce himself; even this would not increase his obscene status.

Poem 89

Gellius is thin, and the poet tells us that this is the result of his ceaseless sexual activity with close relatives. Once again, we have a poem which is rude without primary obscenities, and, once again, Catullus introduces a novel twist at the end. Saying that a man is thin because he overindulges in sex is one thing, saying that he commits incest is another: Catullus argues that Gellius inverts the normal taboo and will *only* have sex with relatives, but that he commits incest on so lavish a scale that he maintains his slender physique.

1   **quid ni**? is a colloquial question: 'how could he not be [thin]?' For the phrasing, cf. 79.1.

2–3   **tam** is repeated five times here to hammer home the generous household of Gellius. **bona** and **bonus** here must mean 'obliging' or 'generous' with their favours (as at 110.1): the mother gives him sex (according to poem 88) and the uncle lets him have his wife (according to poem 74). The sister is **valens** ('vigorous') and also **venusta** – a term deriving from the goddess Venus, which connotes 'attractive' and also 'charming', being used of the poet's home Sirmio (31.12), of men (22.2, 97.9) and of poetry (35.17): *venustas* is missing in unattractive women (86.3) and Varus' girl is 'not *invenustum*' at 10.4. The subjunctive **vivat** (here as at 8.10, 10.33) meaning 'spends her life being') after **cui** shows that this is a 'characteristic' relative clause with causal force (' since he has . . .': see AG §535e).

3–4 **tamque . . . omnia plena** with the ablative is a nice generalisation and takes its point from the emphatically enjambed **cognatis** in the next line: 'the world is so full of girls – and they are *related* to him'. The rhetorical question **quare . . .?** rounds off the first four lines with a reference back to **quid ni** in line 1: **quare desinat** is then a simple potential subjunctive ('why should he stop . . .?')

5 **ut** is concessive: 'although he may touch nothing except that which is forbidden to touch'. The elision of the opening syllable of the line (**qui ut**), not uncommon in Catullus, is rare in later poetry. **attingat** has the sense of 'laying hands on' in a sexual sense, as at 67.20.

6 The reader is invited to look with the second-person verb **invenies**, and then **quare sit macer** ('why he is thin') is the indirect question which will be answered. **quantumvis** (literally, 'as much as you wish') here goes with the whole line: 'you will find as much evidence as you could wish for [to explain] why [Gellius] is thin'.

Poem 91

This poem concludes the four Gellius poems (albeit at greater length and with a gentler tone) but introduces the poet's own beloved and gives us some context for the personal animosity between the men: Gellius, it seems, had stolen Catullus' girl (line 6). The tone is sardonic: the poet's girlfriend was not a blood relation of Gellius and so should have safe from him, and Gellius would not betray his friend. The scornful disappointment is eloquently expressed, with Gellius' joy (**gaudium**) contrasted with Catullus' sorrow (**misero**), the long years of friendship (7) being tossed aside in a compressed half line (**tu satis id duxti**). What makes the poem even more effective is the latent self-criticism. As in poems 8 and 11, the poet casts himself as a good man badly treated, but one has to wonder why he is so surprised that this amoral Gellius should steal the **gaudium** the poet wanted for himself. If Gellius is a villain, then the poet was a fool. Furthermore, the woman he loved was, it seems, very much the driving force of the relationship (e.g. 8.9, 11.17–24, 70, 72, 107) and even Gellius would not seduce her unless she wanted him to – in which case, the poet's anger ought to be directed also at her.

1–6   non ideo … quod … sed … structures the first six lines of the poem: 'not because I knew that you … but rather …'.

1–2   fore is the shortened form of *futurum esse* (future infinitive of *sum*) in indirect statement after **sperabam**. Line 2 is remarkable for the number of elisions (**miser(o) hoc nostr(o) hoc perdit(o) amore**) and the assonance of 'o' which adds to the effect of the poet's howling grief. **miser** means 'lovesick' here as at 8.1, 30.5, 51.5, 64.71, 68.14, 76.19. **perdito** has the sense here of 'ruinous' or 'desperate' love but the word can also mean 'morally depraved' (cf. 42.14) as well as the root meaning of 'lost' (as in 8.2).

3   cognossem is the shortened form of *cognovissem* (pluperfect subjunctive of *cognosco*). The subjunctive is used here and in **putarem** to show that these were not the real reasons for Catullus' expectations (**sperabam**): his real reason is revealed in the indicative **videbam** in line 5. **bene** goes with **cognossem**.

4   This line is indirect statement dependent on te … putarem. The key words **turpi** and **probro** are placed emphatically at the ends of each half of the line and **nec posse … mentem inhibere** almost excuses Gellius' behaviour as being beyond his control.

5   This line repeats the accusations of poems 88–90: the hyperbaton of neque quod (when the sense is *quod neque*) is deliberate: *quod nec* would have scanned equally well.

6   cuius is an objective genitive ('[my] love for whom'). The metaphor of love as 'eating' away at the lover is wonderful: see 35.15, Virgil *Aeneid* 4.66 and may derive from Homer's description of grief 'eating one's heart out' (e.g. Homer *Odyssey* 9.75, *Iliad* 24.129). The metaphor is all the more striking after the crude prosaic accusations of the previous line: Catullus is a man of fine feelings, whereas his adversary is an incestuous brute.

7–8 The poet's provocative language suggests that their long association (**multo usu**) makes Gellius *more* likely to be treacherous: Gellius only goes for relatives – but he and the poet have been in a relationship for a long time – therefore he may go for Catullus' girl. **coniungerer usu** is a phrase which can connote 'common-law' marriage (Treggiari, *Roman Marriage*, pp. 17–21) as well as the less specific 'connected by long familiarity' and so is well chosen for this sentence. **quamvis** (like **ut** in 89.5) commonly takes the subjunctive in this sort of concessive clause. **causae** is a partitive genitive with **satis** ('enough [of] reason'), as is **aliquid sceleris** in line 10.

9   duxti is a shortened form of *duxisti*, from *duco* meaning here 'think'.

10   culpa is stressed by enjambement: it and **sceleris** frame the final line with two sorts of wickedness. The difference between the two words is that **culpa** is a shameful offence (68.139, Virgil *Aeneid* 4.19), whereas **scelus** is more generally a wicked deed (64.397, 67.24, 88.7).

Poem 107

Lesbia has come back to the poet and the text celebrates his unexpected happiness here and in 109. The poem conveys excitement with verbal repetitions and elisions, a gasping hiatus in line 1, and a bumpy metrical rhythm in lines 5 and 7. The style is expressive of the mood, as this eloquent wordsmith finds himself repeating words and phrases, over and over, in a state of almost baffled stupefaction at his own good fortune. Other poems in the collection (e.g. 5, 7) mirror the happiness, while others also show the disillusion setting in (70) and the heartbreak of the relationship's end (8, 11, 76).

The structure is similar to that of 88: eight lines divided into two halves, with repetition of the key phrase at the join (**restituis . . . cupido**) and the word **cupido** (at the end of line 4) marking the close of the section by recalling the same word in line 1.

1   si quicquam is also found as an opening phrase in poems 96 and 102. **optigit** is the perfect tense of *optingo* and sets up a nice jingle after **optantique**. The text requires a hiatus at the caesura (whereby **cupido** does not elide into the first syllable of **optantique**), which might suggest the emotional excitement of the poet, as does the assonance of 'o': perhaps, however, the word -*que* after **cupido** dropped out, as -*que* was often abbreviated (as 'q.') by scribes and easily overlooked. The intensity of the poet's longing for Lesbia is well conveyed in the twin words **cupido optantique**.

2   insperanti is the dative singular of the present participle – 'to one not expecting it' – and is stressed by enjambement. **proprie** here goes with **gratum** and must mean 'truly' or 'fully'.

3   gratum is repeated from line 2. **auro** is an ablative of comparison: '(dearer) than gold'. **nobis** is to be taken with both the adjectives **gratum** and **carius**.

4   quod picks up **hoc** from line 3 and unpacks it: 'this – namely the fact that . . .'. **cupido** repeats the same word from line 1 and is repeated again in the next line. **mi** is the shortened form of *mihi*.

5   insperanti is repeated from line 2. **ipsa refers te** is metrically inelegant – hexameters do not commonly end with monosyllables other than *est* – and may suggest the poet's excitement, as in line 7.

6   nobis here means simply 'to me', and the juxtaposition of **te/nobis** over the line-end is also significant in terms of their new-found closeness (and frequent separation). **o lucem** is an accusative of exclamation, and **candidiore nota** is an ablative of description: 'oh day with a whiter mark'. *lux* (literally 'light') is common in the sense of 'day' (cf. 5.5, 64.16, 64.31), but is also used by the poet of his girlfriend herself ('light of my life') in poem 68.132, 160. Marking a good day with a white pebble is a popular idiom akin to the English 'red-letter day', cf. 68.148, Horace *Odes* 1.36.10.

7–8   The final couplet is framed by **quis ... quis?** **uno** here (as at 10.17) has the sense of 'above all others'. The text of these lines is corrupt and the words printed make sense but are not the finest poetry: 'who lives more fortunate than me above others, and who will be able to talk of things more to be desired than this life?' **vivit** in connection with **vita** retains more of its primary sense 'lives a life'.

Vocabulary

An asterisk * denotes a word in OCR's Defined Vocabulary List for AS.

This vocabulary lists every word in the text. A long single vowel is marked with a macron (e.g. **aetās**), while a short single vowel is marked ˘ in those cases where it is essential to distinguish two similar words (e.g. **dĭcō** and **dīcō**). Nouns are listed with their genitive singular, and verbs are listed with all their four principal parts. Adjectives are listed with the endings of the different genders (e.g. **bonus -a -um**), except where the three genders are the same in the nominative where the genitive is listed (e.g. **potens, potentis**). This vocabulary also lists the places where words occur so that students may quickly compare and contrast the poet's use of each word in different contexts.

*a, ab (+*ablative*)	away from, by
abiciō, abicere, abiēcī, abiectum	to throw aside (88.2)
abluō, abluere, abluī, ablūtum	to wash away (88.6)
abstulit *see* auferō	
absūmō, absūmere, absumpsī, absumptum	to wear out, waste away (64.242)
abūtor, abūti, abūsus sum (+*ablative*)	to abuse (76.4)
*ac	and
*aciēs, aciēī, f.	gaze (64.127)
*ad (+ *accusative*)	to, towards
adeō, adīre, adī(v)i, aditum	to approach (8.16)
*ades	imperative form of **adsum** (62.5, etc.)
*adipīscor, adipīscī, adeptus sum	to obtain (62.57)
adservō, adservāre, adservāvī, adservātum	to protect, look after (17.16)
*adsum, adesse, adfuī	to be present (62.1)

adventō, adventāre, adventāvī, adventātum	to approach, draw near (64.195)
adventus, adventūs, m.	arrival, approach (62.33)
adversus -a -um	facing, opposite (64.128)
advocō, advocāre, advocāvī, advocātus	to summon, invoke (40.3)
Aegēus -ī, m.	Aegeus (father of Theseus)
aequālis -e	comrade, companion (62.11)
aequor, aequoris, n.	sea (11.8, 64.179, 206)
*aequus -a -um	right, fair (62.60)
aereus -a -um	airy (64.240)
āerius -a -um	of the air (64.142)
aes, aeris, n.	money (10.8), bronze (64.262)
aestimō, aestimāre, aestimāvī, aestimātum	to reckon, evaluate (5.3)
aestuōsus -a -um	sweltering (7.5)
aestus -ūs, m.	swelling (of the sea: 64.127)
aetās, aetātis, f.	time (64.237, 76.5)
aevum -ī, n.	historical time (1.6)
agnoscō, agnoscere, agnōvī, agnitum	to recognise (64.237)
*agō, agere, ēgī, actum	to drive (40.2), lead (a life: 76.19)
agricola -ae, m.	farmer (34.19, 62.55)
āles, alitis, m./f.	bird (64.152)
alga -ae, f.	seaweed (64.168)
aliō . . . aliō (*adverbial*)	in one direction . . . in another direction (62.15)
*aliquis, aliquid	someone, something (91.10)
*alius, alia, aliud	another (64.251), other (64.261)
alnus -ī, f.	alder tree (17.18)
Alpes, Alpium, f.	the Alps (11.9)
*alter, altera, alterum	another (5.8–9)
*altus -a -um	high (11.9)
āmēns, āmentis	out of one's mind, mad (64.197)
*amittō, amittere, amīsī, amissum	to lose (virginity 62.46), (a family member 64.150)
amnis -is, m.	stream (34.12)
*amō, amāre, amāvī, amātum	to love
*amor, amōris, m.	love (11.21, 64.182, 76.6, 91.2, 6), love affair (7.8)

amōrēs, amōrum, m. pl.	beloved one (6.16, 10.1, 40.7)
amplius (*adverb*)	more, further (76.10)
*an	or
anguīnus -a -um	snaky (of hair: 64.193)
*animus -ī, m.	mind, heart (62.17, 64.145, 250, 76.11, 107.2)
annuō, annuere, annuī, annūtum	to nod agreement (64.204, 230)
annuus -a -um	yearly (34.18)
*ante (*adverb*)	previously (62.28)
* ante . . . quam (*conjunction*)	before (64.188–90)
antenna -ae, f.	yard-arm (of a ship: 64.234)
antīquē (*adverb*)	in olden times (34.23)
anxius -a -um	anxious, fearful (64.203, 242)
apīscor, apīscī, aptus sum	to obtain (64.145)
*appāreō, apparēre, appāruī, appāritum	to appear (64.168)
*aqua -ae, f.	water (70.4)
*āra -ae, f.	altar (64.132)
Arabes, Arabum, m.	Arabians (11.5)
arātrum -ī, n.	plough (11.24, 62.40)
ardēns, ardēntis	blazing with passion (62.23, 64.124, 197)
ardor, ardōris, m.	flash, gleam (62.29.
argūtātiō, argūtātiōnis, f.	creaking (of a bed:6.11)
Ariadna, -ae, f.	Ariadne (64.253)
āridus -a -um	dry (1.2)
artus -ūs, m.	limb (76.21)
arvum -ī, n.	field (62.49)
arx, arcis, f.	citadel (64.241)
as, assis, m.	penny (small coin:5.3)
aspiciō, aspicere, aspexī, aspectum	to look at, regard (62.12, 76.19)
assiduus -a -um	constant (64.242)
*at	but (64.178)
*atque	and
attingō, attingere, attigī, attactum	to touch (89.5)
attrītus -a -um (*perfect participle of attero*)	worn away (6.10)
auctus -a -um (*perfect participle of augeo*)	endowed with (64.165)
*audeō, audēre, ausus sum	to dare (1.5)

*audiō, audīre, audīvi, audītum	to hear
*aufero, auferre, abstulī, ablātum	to steal, remove (62.32)
aura -ae, f.	breeze (62.41, 64.164)
Aurēlius, -ī, m.	Aurelius (friend of Catullus 11.1)
auris -is, f.	ear (62.15, 64.170)
aurum -ī, n.	gold (107.3)
*aut	or
*aut ... aut ...	either ... or ... (76.7–8)
*autem	on the other hand, meanwhile (64. 167, 207)
*auxilium -ī, n.	help (64.180)
āvehō, āvehere, āvexī, āvectum	to carry off (64.132)
āvellō, avellere, avulsī, avulsum	to tear away (62.21–2)
axulus -ī, m.	timber, plank (17.3)
bacchor, bacchārī, bacchātus sum	to rave (like a Bacchant: 64.255)
barbarus -a -um	foreign (64.264)
bāsiātiō, bāsiātiōnis, f.	kiss, 'kissification' (7.1)
bāsiō, bāsiāre, bāsiāvī, bāsiātum	to kiss (7.9, 8.18)
bāsium -ī, n.	kiss (5.7, 7.9)
Battus -ī, m.	Battus (founder of Cyrene: 7.6)
beātus -a -um	fortunate (10.17)
bellus -a -um	pretty (8.16)
*bene (*adverb of* bonus)	well (10.32, 40.3, 76.7, 91.3)
benefactum -ī, n.	good deed (76.1)
bīmulus -a -um	two-year-old (17.13)
Bīthȳnia -ae, f.	Bithynia (Roman province: 10.7)
blandus -a -um	charming, soothing (64.139)
bombus -ī, m.	booming sound (64.263)
*bona -ōrum, n.	goods (34.19)
*bonus -a -um	good (6.15, 11.16, 17.5, 34.23), generous (89.1–3)
*brevis -e	short, brief (5.5)
Britannus -ī, m.	a Briton (native of Britain: 11.12)
cacūmen, cacūminis, n.	peak, summit (64.240)
*cadō, cadere, cecidī, cāsum	to fall down (11.22)
caecus -a -um	blind (64.197), blinding (64.207)
*caedēs -is, f.	bloodshed, slaughter (64.181)
caeles, caelitis, m.	a god (11.14)
caelestēs, caelestum, m./f. pl.	the gods (64.191, 204)

*caelum -ī, n.	the sky (6.17, 62.20)
caenum -ī, n.	mud (17.25)
Caesar, Caesaris, m.	Gaius Julius Caesar (11.10)
cālīgō, cālīginis, f.	darkness (64.207)
candidus -a -um	bright (8.3), white (64.235, 107.6), beautiful (64.162)
cānitiēs, -iēī, f.	white hair (64.224)
*canō, canere, cecinī, cantum	to sing (34.4, 62.9)
cantus -ūs, m.	sound (of instruments: 64.264)
capillus -ī, m.	hair (64.193)
*capiō, capere, cēpī, captum	to capture (62.24)
*caput, capitis, n.	head (10.11, 17.9; 64.255, 88.8)
carbasus -ī, f.	sailcloth (64.227)
carīna -ae, f.	ship (64.249)
carpō, carpere, carpsī, carptum	to criticise (62.36–7), to pluck (62.43)
carta -ae, f.	roll (of papyrus: 1.6)
*cārus -a -um	dear to ((+ *dative*) 62.45, 47, 58), precious (64.220, 107.3)
castus -a -um	pure, chaste (62.23, 46)
cāsus -ūs, m.	risk, chance event (64.216)
Catullus -ī, m.	Catullus
*causa -ae, f.	reason, cause (91.8)
cavus-a-um	hollow (17.4, 64.259)
Cecropius -a -um	Athenian (64.172)
*cēdō, cēdere, cessī, cessum	to depart (64.249)
celebrō, celebrāre, celebrāvi, celebrātum	to throng in honour of (64.259)
*cēlō, cēlāre, cēlāvī, cēlātum	to hide (64.175)
*centum	100 (5.7–9)
*cernō, cernere, crēvī, crētum	to see (62.6, 64.236), to decide (64.150)
*certē (*adverb*)	certainly (10.14, 62.8, 64.149)
ceu	just like (64.239)
Charybdis -is, f.	Charybdis (a whirlpool: 64.156)
cieō, ciēre, cīvī, citum	to produce (sobs 64.139), (sounds 64.262)
cinaedus -a -um	promiscuous, debauched (10.24)
*cingō, cingere, cīnxī, cīnctum	to encircle, surround (64.185)
Cinna -ae, m.	C. Helvius Cinna (10.30)

cista -ae, f.	wicker-basket (64.259)
***clāmō, clāmāre, clāmāvī, clāmātum**	to shout (metaphorically: 6.7)
clārisonus -a -um	clear-sounding (64.125)
classis -is, f.	fleet (64.212)
clēmentia -ae, f.	compassion (64.137)
***cōgitō, cōgitāre, cōgitāvī,** cōgitātum	to reflect, think (76.2)
cognātus -a -um	related (by blood: 89.4)
***cognōscō, cognoscere, cognōvī,** cognitum	to get to know someone (91.3)
***cōgō, cōgere, coēgi, coactum**	to compel (64.197, 216)
***cohors, cohortis, f.**	the staff (of a provincial governor: 10.10, 13)
collis -is, m.	hill (64.233)
collocō, collocāre, collocāvī, collocātum	to hold in place (10.23)
collum -ī, n.	neck (10.23)
***colō, colere, coluī, cultum**	to cultivate, tend (62.53, 55), to inhabit (64.184)
colōnia -ae, f.	colony (town settled with Roman citizens, 17.1)
colōrō, colōrāre, colōrāvī, colōrātum	to stain, darken (11.7)
***comes, comitis, m.**	companion (11.1)
commodō, commodāre, commodāvī, commodātum	to lend (10.26)
***comparō, comparāre, comparāvī,** comparātum	to acquire, get (10.15)
complector, complectī, complexus sum	to embrace (11.18, 64.214)
complexus -ūs, m.	embrace (62.21–2)
comprecor, comprecārī, comprecātus sum	to pray for (64.191)
comprendō, comprendere, comprendī, comprensum	to overtake, catch (62.35)
concēdō, concēdere, concessī, concessum	to grant, allow (64.228)
concipiō, concipere, concēpī, conceptum	to conceive (64.155)

concrēdō, concrēdere, concrēdidī, concrēditum	to entrust (64.213)
concutiō, concutere, concussī, concussum	to shake (64.206)
*condō, condere, condidī, conditum	to store, keep safe (64.231)
coniungō, coniungere, coniūnxī, coniūnctum	to join (62.54), to unite, connect (91.7)
*coniunx, coniugis, m./f.	spouse (62.59, 64.182)
conqueror, conquerī, conquestus sum	to complain (64.164)
conscendō, conscendere, conscendī, conscēnsum	to climb (64.126)
conserō, conserere, consēvī, consitum	to plant, sow (64.208)
*consilium -ī, n.	purpose, design (64.137, 176)
consōlor, consōlārī, consōlatus sum	to console, comfort (64.182)
*conspiciō, conspicere, conspexī, conspectum	to catch sight of (64.243)
constans, constantis	steadfast (64. 209, 64.238), trustworthy (91.3)
consternō, consternere, constrāvī, constrātum	to spread (a couch 64.163)
consurgō, consurgere, consurrexī, consurrectum	to stand up, rise (62.1,6)
contingō, contingere, contigī, contactum	to touch (62.52)
*contrā (adverbial)	to face them (62.6), in return (76.23)
contremescō, contremescere, contremuī	to tremble (64.205)
conturbō, conturbāre, conturbāvī, conturbātum	to muddle the accounts (5.11)
cōnūbium -ī, n.	marriage (62.27, 57: 64.101, 158)
convellō, convellere, convellī, convulsum	to uproot, tear out (62.40)
convertō, convertere, convertī, conversum	to direct, turn (62.17)
cor, cordis, n.	heart (64.124, 231)

cordī esse (+*dative*)	to be pleasing to (64.158)
Cornēlius -ī, m.	Cornelius Nepos (1.3)
cornū -ūs, n.	horn (musical instrument 64.263)
***corpus, corporis, n.**	body (62.46, 62.51, 64.189)
***crēdō, crēdere, crēdidī, crēditum**	to trust (64.143), to believe (64.245,
(+ *dative*)	91.8), to invest in (76.9)
Crēta -ae, f.	Crete (64.174)
crēvī *see* **cernō**	
***crūdēlis, -e**	cruel, harsh (62.20, 24: 64.136, 175)
crūs, crūris, n.	leg (upright support of a bridge: 17.3)
cubīle -is, n.	bed (6.7, 64.163)
***culpa -ae, f.**	fault, wrongdoing (11.22, 91.10)
***cum (+ *ablative*)**	with (11.17, 62.59–65, 64.252, 89.1), at
	risk of (40.8)
***cum (+ *indicative*)**	when (1.5, 5.5, 7.7, 8.4–6, 62.43, 62.57,
	76.2)
***cum (+ *subjunctive*)**	since (5.13), although (17.14), when
	(64.212-3)
***cum primum**	as soon as (64.243)
***cuncta (n. pl. of cunctus -a -um)**	everything (64.142, 64.208)
***cupidus -a -um**	lustful, desirous (64.147, 70.3, 107.1,
	107.4–5)
***cupiō, cupīre, cupī(v)ī, cupītum**	to long for, desire (17.1, 64.145,
	64.260)
***cūr**	why (10.11, 76.10)
***cūra -ae, f.**	diligence, hard work (62.16), care,
	worries (64.250)
cūriōsus -a -um	inquisitive, nosy (7.11)
***cūrō, cūrāre, cūrāvi, cūrātum**	to care about (64.148)
cursus -ūs, m.	course, journey (34.17)
cuspis, cuspidis, f.	spear-tip, spike (64.256)
custōdia -ae, f.	guard-post (62.33)
Cyrēnae, Cyrēnārum, f. pl.	Cyrene (7.4)
***dē (+ *ablative*)**	down from (17.8, 17.23)
***dea -ae, f.**	goddess (34.17, 64.201)
decet, decēre, decuit (*impersonal*	it is fitting, appropriate (10.24, 62.18)
***verb+ accusative*)**	
***dēfendō, dēfendere, dēfendī,**	to defend (64.229)
dēfēnsum	

dēferō, dēferre, dētulī, dēlātum	to convey, carry (10.27)
dēflectō, dēflectere, dēflexī, dēflectum	to bend downwards (62.51)
dēflōrescō, dēflōrescere, dēflōruī	to shed petals 62.43)
*dein/deinde	then, next (5.7–10)
dēlicātus -a -um	wanton, frisky (17.15)
dēliciae, dēliciārum, f.	sweetheart, girlfriend (6.1)
Dēlius -a -um	on the island of Delos (34.7)
dēmittō, dēmittere, dēmīsī, dēmissum	to lower, drop (88.8)
dēpōnō, dēpōnere, dēposuī/ dēposīvi, dēpositum	to give birth to (34.8), to lower (64.234), to cast off, get rid of (76.13, 76.25)
dērelinquō, dērelinquere, dērelīquī, dērelictum	to leave behind (17.25)
desertus -a -um	deserted (64.137, 187)
*dēsinō, dēsinere, dēsī(v)ī, dēsitum (+ infinitive)	to stop (8.1, 76.12, 89.4)
dēspondeō, dēspondēre, dēspondī, dēsponsum	to pledge (62.27)
dēstinātus -a -um	resolute, firm (8.19)
dēsum, dē(e)sse, dēfuī (+ dative)	to fail someone (64.151)
*deus, deī, m (ablative pl.: dis (76.12))	god (40.3)
dēvōtus -a -um	accursed (64.135)
*dextra, -ae, f.	right hand (64.230)
*dī, deōrum, m. pl.	gods (76.17, 76.26)
Diāna -ae, f.	Diana (goddess: 34.1–3)
dĭcō, dĭcāre, dĭcāvi, dĭcātum	to indicate (64.227)
*dīcō, dīcere, dīxī, dictum	to talk, speak (6.3, 6.16), to say (8.17, 10.15, 10.28, 64.130, 70.1–3, 76.7–8, 107.8), to call (34.14–16), to sing (62.5, 62.18)
dicta, dictōrum, n. pl.	words (11.16, 64.148)
*difficilis, -e	difficult (76.13–14)
dīlacerō, dīlacerāre, dīlacerāvī, dīlacerātum	to tear to pieces (64.152)
*dīligens, dīligentis	careful (17.16)
dīligō, dīligere, dīlexī, dīlectum	to love (6.5, 76.23)

*dīmittō, dīmittere, dīmīsī, dīmissum	to dismiss (64.208), to send away (64.216)
*dīrus -a -um	dreadful (64.173)
*dīs (76.12) *see* deus	
*discēdō, discēdere, discessī, discessum	to leave, depart (64.134)
discernō, discernere, discrēvī, discrētum	to separate, divide off (64.179)
discerpō, discerpere, discerpsī, discerptum	to tear to shreds (64.142)
*diū (*adverb*)	for a long time (62.2)
dīva -ae, f.	goddess (64.212)
dīvellō, dīvellere, dīvulsī, dīvulsum	to tear to pieces (64.257)
*dīvidō, dīvidere, dīvīsī, dīvīsum	to divide (62.15), to separate (64.179)
dīvus -ī, m. (gen. pl. dīvum: 76.4, 64.134)	god (62.30, 64.190)
*dō, dare, dedī, datum	to give (5.7, 17.7, 62.30, 62.63–5, 64.139, 152, 214)
doctus -a -um	scholarly (1.7)
*doleō, dolēre, doluī, dolitum	to grieve, lament (8.14), to be in pain (34.13)
*domina -ae, f.	mistress (34.9)
*domum (*accusative of* domus)	homewards (64.135)
*domus -ūs/ī, f.	home (64.246)
dōnō, dōnāre, dōnāvī, dōnātum	to hand over, give to (1.1, 62.23)
*dormiō, dormīre, dormiī/ dormīvī, dormītum	to sleep (5.6, 17.13)
dōs, dōtis, f.	dowry (62.65)
*dubius -a -um	dangerous, perilous (64.216)
*dūcō, dūcere, dūxī, ductum	to lead (8.4), to bring (10.2, 64.160), to think (8.2, 91.9)
dulcis, -e	precious (64.157), attractive (64.175), welcome (64.210)
*dum (*conjunction* + *indicative*)	while, so long as (62.45, 62.56, 64.145)
*duo, duae, duo	two (62.64)
*e, ex (+*ablative*)	from out of (64.241, 64.251, 76.22), in accordance with (17.5), arising out of (76.6)

ecfutuō, ecfutuere, ecfutuī, ecfutūtum	to wear out with too much sex (6.13)
ecquid (*interrogative particle*)	surely? (88.4)
edō, esse, ēdī, ēsum	to eat away at, consume (91.6)
ēdŭcō, ēdŭcāre, ēdŭcāvī, ēdŭcātum	to nurture (62.41), produce (62.50)
efferō, efferre, extulī, ēlātum	to raise on high (62.29)
*efficiō, efficere, effēcī, effectum	to achieve, bring about (76.14)
efflō, efflāre, efflāvī, efflātum	to blare out (64.263)
*ego, meī	I (*personal pronoun*: 10.16, 10.31, 64.149, 64.164, 64.196, 64.216, 64.221)
egressus -ūs, m.	escape (64.185)
*eō, īre, iī/īvī, itum	to go, fall (17.4, 17.9)
Eōus -a -um	Eastern (11.3)
Eōus (*masculine of* Eōus *as noun*)	the morning star (62.35)
Erechthēus -a -um	Athenian (64.211
Erectheus, Erectheī, m.	Erectheus (64.229)
ēripiō, ēripere, ēripuī, ēreptum	to rescue (64.150), to snatch away (64.219) to take away (76.20)
*et	and
*etiam (*particle*)	even (64.170)
euhoe	'euhoe' (ritual cry of Bacchants: 64.255)
eum *see* is	
Eumenidēs, Eumenidum, f. pl.	The Eumenides, Furies (64.193)
*ex (*see* e, ex)	
*excitō, excitāre, excitāvī, excitātum	to awaken (17.24), to provoke (40.4)
excruciō, excruciāre, excruciāvī, excruciātum	to torture, torment (76.19, 85.2)
expellō, expellere, expulī, expulsum	to drive out (76.22)
expleō, explēre, explēvī, explētum (+ *ablative*)	to fill up with (34.20)
explicō, explicāre, explicāvī, explicātum	to explain, unfold (1.6)
expoliō, expolīre, expoliī/īvī, expolītum	to polish (1.2)
exposcō, exposcere, expoposcī	to demand (64.190), beg for (64.203)

exprōmō, exprōmere, exprompsī, expromptum	to utter, express (64.223)
exsiliō, exsilīre, exsiluī	to leap up (62.8–9)
*exspectō, exspectāre, exspectāvī, exspectātum	to await, expect (62.2)
exspīrō, exspīrāre, exspīrāvī, exspīrātum (*intransitive*)	to be exhaled, to blast out (64.194)
exspuō, exspuere, exspuī, exspūtum	to spit out (64.155)
externō, externāre, externāvī, externātum	to drive mad (64.165)
extollō, extollere	to raise (62.50)
extrēmus -a -um	furthest (11.2), desperate (64.130, 64.169), final (64.217, 76.18), deepest (64.196)
extulit (62.29: *see* efferō)	
*facilis -e	easy (62.11)
*faciō, facere, fēcī, factum	to do (6.14, 62.24, 76.8, 76.16, 85.1, 88.1–3), to reach a total (5.10), to render (10.17)
facitō ut	see to it that (64.231)
pilī facere	to care a jot for (10.13, 17.17)
*factum -ī, n. (*perfect participle of* faciō)	deed (64.192, 64.203)
fallax, fallācis	treacherous, deceitful (64.151)
*fallō, fallere, fefellī, falsum	to deceive (76.4)
famulor, famulārī, famulātus sum	to serve (64.161)
fās (*indeclinable neuter noun*)	that which is right by divine law (89.5)
fascinō, fascināre, fascināvī, fascinātum	to bewitch, cast a spell on (7.12)
fateor, fatērī, fassus sum	to admit (6.5)
fātum -ī, n.	fate, doom (64.245)
febrīculōsus -a -um	feverish, sickly (6.4)
*fēlix, felīcis	happy (62.30), fortunate (107.7)
*fēmina -ae, f.	woman (64.143)
*ferō, ferre, tulī, lātum	to bring (11.13, 64.173, 76.18), to bear (64.222), to say, allege (64.212)
*feror, ferrī (*passive of* ferō)	to travel, ride (62.20)
*ferox, ferōcis	fierce (64.247)

ferreus -a -um	made of iron (17.26)
ferrūgō, ferrūginis, f.	colour of rust (64.227)
ferus -ī, m.	wild beast (64.152)
fervidus -a -um	blazing, passionate (64.218)
fessus -a -um	weary (64.189)
fictus -a -um	fake, false (62.36)
*fidēlis -e	reliable, trustworthy (64.144)
*fidēs, -ēī, f.	protection (64.191), good faith, trust (76.3)
in fidē (+ *genitive*)	under the care of (34.1)
fīdus -a -um	faithful (64.182, 91.1)
figūra -ae, f.	appearance (64.220)
*fīnis -is, m./f.	limit (64.217)
*fīō, fierī, factus sum	to be done (8.6, 76.8, 85.2), to be made (17.5)
firmō, firmāre, firmāvī, firmātum	to confirm (62.27), to strengthen (62.41)
flagellum -ī, n.	tendril (62.52)
flāmen, flāminis, n.	blast, gust (of winds: 64.239)
*flamma -ae, f.	flame (62.27)
Flāvius -ī, m.	Flavius (6.1)
flectō, flectere, flexī, flexum	to deflect, turn aside (64.136)
flētus -ūs, m.	weeping (64.242)
flōreō, flōrēre, flōruī	to be vigorous (64.251)
flōs, flōris, m.	flower (11.23, 62.39), youthful prime (17.14), virginity (62.46)
foedō, foedāre, foedāvī, foedātum	to stain, defile (64.224)
*foedus, foederis, n.	agreement (76.3)
*fore = futurum esse (*future infinitive of* sum: 91.2)	
*forem = essem (*imperfect subjunctive of* sum: 34.9)	
forma -ae, f.	appearance (64.175)
fors, fortis, f.	fortune (64.170)
*fortasse	perhaps (85.1)
*forte	by chance (62.54)
*fortūna -ae, f.	misfortune (64.218), fortune (64.222)
*forum -ī, n.	forum (central area of a town: 10.2)
fossa -ae, f.	ditch (17.19)

frāgrans, frāgrantis	sweet-smelling (6.8)
*frangō, frangere, frēgī, fractum	to break (10.22)
frāternus -a -um	belonging to a brother (64.181)
frīgidulus -a -um	chilly, cold (64.131)
frons, frontis, f.	forehead, brow (64.194)
*frustrā	in vain (62.13)
frux, frūgis, f.	crop (34.20)
*fuga -ae, f.	escape (64.186)
*fugiō, fugere, fūgī	to run away, flee (8.10, 64.183)
fūgit mē ratio	I made a mistake (10.29)
fulgeō, fulgēre, fulsī	to shine (8.3, 8.8)
*fundō, fundere, fūdī, fūsum	to pour out (64.125)
fūnestō, fūnestāre, fūnestāvī, fūnestātum	to pollute, ruin (64.201)
fūnestus -a -um	mournful (64.234, 64.246)
fūnis -is, m.	mooring rope, hawser (64.174)
fūr, fūris, m.	thief, robber (62.34)
furens, furentis	frenzied (64.124)
Fūrius -ī, m.	Marcus Furius Bibaculus (11.1)
furō, furere	to rave, to be crazed (64.254)
*furor, furōris, m.	madness (64.197)
furtīvus -a -um	secret, stealthy (7.8)
Gāius, -ī, m.	Gaius Helvius Cinna (10.30)
Gallicus -a -um	Gallic, in Gaul (11.11)
*gaudeō, gaudēre, gāvīsus sum	to be happy (64.221)
*gaudium –(i)ī, n.	joy, delight (64.236. 76.6, 91.9)
Gellius –(i)i, m.	L. Gellius Poplicola (88.1, 88.5, 89.1, 91.1)
gener, generī, m.	son-in-law (62.65)
genitor, genitōris, m.	father (88.6)
*gens, gentis, f.	race (34.24)
*genus, generis, n.	people, race (64.229)
germāna -ae, f.	sister (91.5)
germānus -ī, m.	brother (64.150)
gignō, gignere, genuī, genitum	to give birth to (64.154)
Gnōsius -a -um	Cretan (64.172)
grabātus -ī, m.	camp bed, couch (10.22)
gradior, gradī, gressus sum	to march (11.9)
grātus -a -um	welcome, pleasing (107.2-3)

*gravis -e	heavy, thick (17.25)
gurges, gurgitis, m.	a mass of water, sea (178, 183)
*habeō, habēre, habuī, habitum	to have (6.15, 10.28, 17.2, 62.13)
se habēre	to fare (10.7)
haedus -ī, m.	kid, young goat (17.15)
harēna -ae, f.	sand (7.3)
Hesperus -ī, m.	Hesperus (the evening star: 62.20, 62.26, 62.32, 62.35)
Hibērus -a -um	Spanish (64.227)
*hīc (adverb)	here (6.9, 10.21), at this point (10.24)
*hic, haec, hoc	this (64.256, 107.7, etc.)
*homō, hominis, m.	man (plural: people) (7.8, 10.16–20, 17.12, 76.2, 76.4–7)
*hōra -ae, f.	hour (62.30, 64.191)
horreō, horrēre, horruī	to dread (64.159)
horribilis -e	dreadful, terrifying (11.11, 64.264)
horridus -a -um	rough, choppy (of waters: 64.205)
*hortus -ī, m.	garden (62.39)
*hospes, hospitis, m.	guest (64.176)
*hostis -is, m.	enemy (62.24)
*hūc (adverb)	to this place (10.5, 64.195)
Hymēn, m.	'Hymen' (ritual refrain chanted at weddings: 62 passim)
Hymenaeus -ī, m.	the processional marriage song (62.4, etc.) a wedding (64.141)
Hyrcānī, -ōrum, m. pl.	The Hyrcanians (11.5)
Iacchus -ī, m.	Bacchus (64.251)
*iaceō, iacēre, iacuī, iacitum	to lie down (6.6, 7.4, 17.19)
*iaciō, iacere, iēcī, iactum	to throw, hurl (64.244)
iactō, iactāre, iactāvī, iactātum	to throw about (64.257)
*iam	now (8.9, 8.12, 10.7, 62.3–4, 62.18, 76.10, 76.23), by now (64.167, 76.18)
iam iam	any time now (62.52)
iam tum	already by then (1.5)
nunc iam	from now on (64.143)
iambus -ī, m.	invective poetry (40.2)
*ibi	there and then (8.6)
Īdaeus -a -um	of Mount Ida (in Crete: 64.178)

*īdem, eadem, idem	the same (62.34, 62.43, 62.54)
identidem	repeatedly, again and again (11.19)
ideō	for this reason (91.1)
*igitur	therefore (62.16)
ignārus -a -um	uncomprehending (64.164)
*ignis -is, m.	fire (62.7), blazing star (62.20, 62.26)
ignōtus -a -um (+ *dative*)	unknown to (62.40)
īlia, īlium, n. pl.	the groin, genitals (11.20)
*ille, illa, illud	that, those (5.11, 8.6–9, 10.31, 76.23), he, she, it (10.24, 11.22, 62.42–4, 62.55, 64.124, 64.167, 76.23)
illepidus -a -um	unsophisticated, unattractive (6.2, 10.4)
*illīc	in that place (6.9, 10.14, 10.21)
imber, imbris, m.	rain-shower (62.41)
immemor, immemoris	heedless, forgetful (64.135, 64.248)
immītis -e	merciless, harsh (64.138, 64.245)
impotens, impotentis	powerless (8.9)
īmus -a -um	inmost, deepest (64.125, 64.198, 76.21)
*in (+ *ablative*)	in, on
*in (+ *accusative*)	into, against
inambulātiō -ōnis, f.	walking, pacing (6.11)
*incendium –(i)ī, n.	fire (*metaphorical*: 64.226)
*incendō, incendere, incendī, incensum	to inflame (64.253)
incidō, incidere, incidī, incāsum	to crop up in talk (10.5), to fall to one's lot (10.19)
incingō, incingere, incīnxī, incīnctum	to wrap (64.258)
*incipiō, incipere, incēpī, inceptum	to begin (62.18)
incola -ae, f.	island (64.184)
incultus -a -um	untended (62.56)
incurvō, incurvāre, incurvāvī, incurvātum	to bend (64.183)
*inde	then (64.225)
indomitus -a -um	untamed, violent (64.173)
Indus -ī, m.	Indian (inhabitant of India: 11.2)

inēlegans, inēlegantis	lacking in charm (6.2)
ineptia -ae, f.	silliness (6.14)
ineptiō, ineptīre	to act foolishly (8.1)
ineptus -a -um	ill-fitting (17.2)
inficiō, inficere, infēcī, infectum	to stain, dye (64.225, 64.243)
inflectō, inflectere, inflexī, inflexum	to bend back, toss (64.255)
infundō, infundere, infūdī, infūsum	to pour on (64.224)
ingrātus -a -um	thankless (76.6), ungrateful (76.9)
*ingredior, ingredī, ingressus sum	to enter (64.246)
inhibeō, inhibēre, inhibuī, inhibitum	to restrain (91.4)
iniciō, inicere, iniēcī, iniectum	to throw on (64.153)
innuptus -a -um	unmarried (62.6, 62.12, 62.36)
inops, inopis	helpless (64.197)
*inquam (perfect: inquiī)	to say (10.14, 10.18, 10.25, 10.27)
īnspērans, īnspērantis	not expecting (107.2, 107.5)
instar (+genitive)	as much as (17.12)
*insula -ae, f.	island (64.184)
insulsus -a -um	boring (10.33), stupid (17.12)
insultō, insultāre, insultāvī, insultātum	to mock, scoff (64.169)
intactus -a -um	untouched (62.45, 62.56)
integer, integra, integrum	unmarried, unsullied (34.2–3)
*inter (+ accusative)	between (7.5)
intorqueō, intorquēre, intorsī, intortum	to twist (64.235)
*inveniō, invenīre, invēnī, inventum	to find (89.6)
invenustus -a -um	unattractive (10.4)
invictus -a -um	unconquered (64.204)
invideō, invidēre, invīdī, invīsum	to look in a hostile way (5.12), to begrudge (64.170)
invīsō, invīsere, invīsī, invīsum	to come to see (64.233)
invīsus -a -um (+ dative)	disliked, odious (62.58)
*invītus -a -um	unwilling, reluctant (8.13, 64.219, 76.12)
iocōsus -a -um	jolly, entertaining (8.6)

*ipse, ipsa, ipsum	himself, herself, itself, themselves (62.60, etc.), natives (10.9), actual (76.18)
*īra -ae, f.	anger (64.194)
irritus -a -um	null and void, empty (64.142)
irrumātor, irrumātōris, m.	a sexually abusive superior (10.12)
*is, ea, id (*third person pronoun*)	him, her, it (17.23, 89.4)
iste, ista, istud	that, those (6.12, 10.26–8, 17.21)
istinc	from that place (76.11)
Italus -a -um	Italian (1.5)
*iter, itineris, n.	journey (34.18)
Itōnus, Itōnī, f.	Itonus (a town in Thessaly: 64.228)
*iubeō, iubēre, iussī, iussum	to urge, tell (64.140)
iūcundus -a -um	attractive (62.26, 62.47), delightful (64.161), pleasing (64.215)
*iungō, iungere, iunxī, iunctum	to join, unite (62.29)
Iūnō, Iūnōnis, f.	Juno (goddess: 34.14)
Iuppiter, Iovis, m.	Jupiter (god: 1.7, 7.5, 34.6, 64.171, 70.2)
iūre (*adverb*)	rightly (62.16)
iūrō, iūrāre, iūrāvī, iūrātum	to swear an oath (64.143, 64.146)
iūs, iūris, n.	(legal) right (62.65)
*iustus -a -um	rightful, just (64.190)
iuvencus -ī, m.	bullock (62.53, 62.55, 64.257)
*iuvenis -is, m.	young man (62.1, 62.6, 62.23, 64.181, 64.214)
labellum -ī, n.	lip (8.18)
*labor, labōris, m.	labour, effort (64.161)
labōriōsus -a -um	involving hard work (1.7)
*labōrō, labōrāre, labōrāvī, labōrātum	to work hard (62.14)
lacus -ūs, m.	pool (17.10)
laetitia -ae, f.	joy, happiness (76.22)
laetor, laetārī, laetātus sum	to be joyful (64.221)
*laetus -a -um	joyful (64.141, 64.236)
languescō, languescere, languī	to grow feeble, weaken (64.188)
languidus -a -um	drooping, weary (64.219)
lāsarpīcifer, -era, -erum	Silphium-bearing (7.4)
lateō, latēre, latuī	to hide, lurk (62.34)

Lātōnia -ae, f.	daughter of Leto (Diana: 34.5)
*lātus -a -um	wide (64.178)
*latus, lateris, n.	flank (6.13)
leaena -ae, f.	lioness (64.154)
lectīca -ae, f.	a litter-chair (10.16)
lectus -ī, m.	bed (6.10)
*lentus -a -um	pliant, sluggish (64.183)
lepidus -a -um	elegant, charming (1.1, 6.17)
Lesbia -ae, f.	Lesbia (5.1, 7.2, 107.4)
lētum -ī, n.	death (64.149, 64.187)
libellus -ī, m.	small book (1.1, 1.8)
libīdō, libīdinis, f.	desire (64.147)
ex tuā libīdine	as you desire (17.5)
Libyssa -ae, f.	of North Africa (7.3)
*licet, licēre, licuit (impersonal verb)	it is permitted, one may (10.34)
Ligus, Liguris	from Liguria (17.19)
lingua -ae, f.	tongue (7.12)
linquō, linquere, līquī	to leave (62.3, 64.213, 64.240), to abandon (64.133)
linteum -ī, n.	sail (64.225, 64.243)
liquidus -a -um	liquid (64.162)
*lītus, lītoris, n.	seashore (11.3, 64.133, 64.172)
līvidus -a -um	greyish-blue (17.11)
*longē (adverb)	afar, over a great distance (11.3)
*longus -a -um	long (in size: 17.1), long-lasting (40.8, 64.215, 76.5, 76.13)
lubet, lubēre, lubuit (impersonal verb)	it pleases (17.17, 62.36, 76.14)
lūceō, lūcēre, lūxī	to shine (62.26)
Lūcīna -ae, f.	Lucina (goddess of childbirth: 34.13)
luctus -ūs, m.	grief, sorrow (64.199, 64.226, 64.247)
lūdō, lūdere, lūsī, lūsum	to have fun (17.1), to play around (17.17)
lūmen, luminis, n.	light (34.16, 62.2), eye (64.188, 64.220, 64.233, 64.242)
Lūna -ae, f.	the moon (34.16)
lutum -ī, n.	mud, clay (17.9)
*lux, lūcis, f.	day (5.5, 107.6)

lympha -ae, f.	water (64.162)
lymphātus -a -um	frenzied, driven mad (64.254)
macer, macra, macrum	thin (89.4, 89.6)
maestus -a -um	sad, mournful (64.130, 64.202, 64.210, 64.249)
*magis (*adverb*)	more (62.59, 107.7)
*magnus -a -um (*superlative*: maximus -a -um)	great (7.3, 11.10, 17.7, 17.11, 34.5–6, 91.6)
malignus -a -um	stingy, mean (10.18)
*mālō, mālle, māluī	to prefer (70.1)
*malus -a -um	evil (5.12, 7.12, 64.175), bad (6.15, 10.19, 10.33), sick (40.1), disastrous (64.165)
mālus -ī, m.	mast (64.225)
mandātum -ī, n.	instruction (64.209, 64.214, 64.232, 64.238)
*maneō, manēre, mānsī, mānsum	to remain (1.10, 62.45–7, 62.56), to await, lie in store (8.15, 76.5), to wait (10.27)
*mare, maris, n.	sea (64.155)
marītus -a -um	'wedded', united (62.54)
*marītus -ī, m.	husband (88.3)
*māter, mātris, f.	mother (34.7, 62.21–2, 61–3, 88.1, 89.1, 91.5)
mātūrus -a -um	proper, due (of time: 62.57)
*mē (*accusative of* ego)	me (10.1, 10.17, 10.28–9, 64.132, 64.177, 64.200, 76.19, 76.23, 91.6, 107.7)
meditor, meditārī, meditātus sum	to think out in advance (a speech, etc.: 62.12–13)
*medius -a -um	the middle of (64.149, 64.167)
medulla -ae, f.	inmost heart (64.196)
membrum -ī, n.	limb (64.257)
mēmet	me (64.182)
memor, memoris	mindful, unforgetting (64.231)
memorābilis -e	remarkable, noteworthy (62.13)
*mēns, mentis, f.	mind (8.11, 62.14–15, 62.37, 64.136, 64.147, 64.207–9, 64.236, 64.238, 91.4), intention (40.1), state of mind (64.200–1, 64.248, 64.254), heart (64.223-6, 76.9)

mēnsa -ae, f.	dining table (62.3)
mēnstruus -a -um	monthly (34.17)
mētior, mētiri, mēnsus sum	to measure (34.18)
metuō, metuere, metuī, metūtum	to be afraid (64.146), be anxious about (64.148)
*meus, mea, meum	my (1.4, 5.1, 10.1, 10.29, 11.15, 11.21, 17.8, 17.21, 40.2, 40.7, 64.195, 64.218, 70.1, 76.26)
*mī (=mihi, *from* ego))	to me (5.7, 10.21, 76.26, 107.4)
*mī (*vocative of* meus)	o my (10.25)
micō, micāre, micāvī, micātum	to gleam (64.206)
*mihi (*dative of* ego)	(to) me (7.1, 10.3, 10.8, 10.18, 10.25, 17.7, 64.140, 64.188, 64.215–17, 70.2, 76.21, 91.1), for myself (10.32), from me (64.219, 76.20)
*mīlle (*plural*: mīlia)	thousand (5.7–10)
Mīnōis, Mīnōidis, f.	daughter of Minos (Ariadne: 64.247)
*minus (*comparative adverb*)	less (62.58)
mīrus -a -um	surprising (62.14)
misellus -a -um (*diminutive of* miser)	pathetic (40.1)
*miser, misera, miserum	unhappy, lovesick (8.1, 8.10, 64.140, 64.196, 76.12, 76.19, 91.2)
misereor, misererī, miserātus sum	to pity (76.17)
miserescō, miserescere (+ *genitive*)	to have compassion towards (64.138)
mītis -e	sweet, juicy (62.50)
*mittō, mittere, mīsī, missum	to send (17.23, 64.221), to utter (64.166)
*modo	just now (1.2, 10.28), *see also* quō . . . modo
moechus -ī, m.	adulterous lover (11.17)
*moenia -ium, n. pl.	city walls (64.212)
molestus -a -um	troublesome, annoying (10.33)
mollis -e	effeminate (11.5), soft (64.129)
monimentum -i, n.	monument, memorial (11.10)
*mōns, mōntis, m.	mountain (34.9, 64.126, 64.178, 64.240)
*morbus -ī, m.	disease (76.25)
mordeō, mordere, momordī, morsum	to bite (8.18)

*mors, mortis, f.	death (64.188, 64.247, 76.18)
mortālis -e	human (64.168)
mortuus -a -um	dead (64.153)
mōtus -ūs, m.	movement (64.205)
mūla -ae, f.	she-mule (17.26)
mulceō, mulcēre, mulsī, mulsum	to caress (62.41)
*mulier -eris, f.	woman (70.1, 70.3)
multa -ae, f.	penalty, punishment (64.190)
multiplex, multiplicis	many at one time, numerous (64.250)
multō, multāre, multāvi, multātum	to punish (64.192)
*multus -a -um	much, many (5.10, 7.7–9, 8.6, 62.42, 62.55, 64.223, 64.263, 76.5, 91.7)
mundus -ī, m.	sky, heavens (64.206)
mūniceps, mūnicipis, m.	a fellow-townsman (17.8)
*mūnus, mūneris, n.	gift, spectacle (17.7)
*mūto, mūtāre, mūtāvī, mūtātum	to change (62.35)
mūtus -a -um	silent (64.186)
*nam	for (6.6, 6.12, 10.26, 64.177, 76.7, 88.7)
namque	for (1.3, 62.33, 64.212)
*nāscor, nāscī, nātus sum	to come into being (62.39, 62.49), to spring up (64.198), to originate (10.15)
nāta -ae, f.	daughter (62.21–2)
nātus -ī, m.	son (64.213–6, 220)
*nāvita -ae, m. (=*nauta*)	sailor (64.174)
*nē (+ *subjunctive*)	so that. . .not (5.11–12), *see also* **utinam nē**
(+*imperative*)	do not (62.59)
nē quis	so that nobody (5.12)
*nec/neque	and not, nor (6.3, 8.7, 8.10, 8.13, 10.4, 10.9–10, 10.13, 11.21, 17.12, 17.17–18, 62.14, 62.29, 64.153, 64.168, 64.173, 64.175, 64.185, 64.189, 64.210, 64.222, 64.232, 88.6)
*nec/neque . . . nec/neque . . .	neither . . . nor . . . (7.11–12, 10.21, 62.47, 64.166, 76.3, 91.5)
*necesse	compulsory (62.61)
neglegēns -ntis	careless (10.34)

*neglegō, neglegere, neglēxī, neglectum	to ignore, disregard (64.134)
*neque see nec	
nēquīquam	in vain, to no purpose (6.7, 64.164)
*nescio, nescīre, nesciī/īvī, nescitum	not to know (17.22, 85.2)
nescioquid (+ *genitive*)	some sort of (6.4)
*nī (= nisi)	unless (6.2, 6.14), *see also* quid ni
niger -gra -grum	black, ripe (17.16)
*nihil/ nīl	nothing (10.9, 17.21, 64.146, 88.7, 89.5), not at all (6.12, 64.148)
Nīlus -ī, m.	Nile (river: 11.8)
nīmīrum	evidently (62.7)
nimis	too much (64.169)
*nisi	except (89.5)
nītor, nītī, nīxus/nīsus sum	to rely on (64.177)
niveus -a -um	snow-capped (64.240)
Noctifer -erī, m.	the evening star (62.7)
*nōlō, nōlle, nōluī	to refuse (8.7, 8.9)
* nōlī, nōlīte (*imperative of* nōlō)	do not (8.9, 62.64, 64.199)
*nōmen -inis, n.	name (34.22, 62.35)
*nōn	not
*nōndum	not yet (64.219)
*nōs, nostrī	we, us (5.5, 6.16, 10.5, 62.11, 62.32, 62.15), me (8.5, 64.138, 107.3, 107.6)
*noster, nostra, nostrum	our (64.158, 64.176, 64.229, 64.233), my (64.170, 64.199, 64.226, 91.2)
nota -ae, f.	sign, mark (107.6)
nothus -a -um	borrowed (34.15)
*nōtus -a -um	well known (40.6)
*novus -a -um	new (1.1)
*nox, noctis, f.	night (5.6, 6.6, 7.7, 62.34)
nūbēs -is, f.	cloud (64.239)
nūbō, nūbere, nūpsī, nūptum	to marry (70.1)
nūdō, nūdāre, nūdāvī, nūdātum	to strip bare (64.129)
nūdus -a -um	bare (of trees: 62.49)
nūgae -ārum, f. pl.	trifles, light efforts (1.4)

nulla (*as adverb*)	not at all (8.14, 17.20)
nullus -a -um (*as noun*)	nobody (8.5, 10.21, 70.1)
*nullus -a -um (*as adjective*)	not any, none (11.19, 62.40, 62.44, 62.53, 64.136–7, 64.143–4, 64.165, 64.184, 64.186, 76.3)
nūmen, nūminis, n.	power (of gods: 64.134, 64.204, 76.4)
*numerus -ī, m.	number (7.3)
*numquam	never (62.50)
*nunc	now (8.9, 8.16–17, 17.23, 62.17), from now on (64.143)
*nuntiō, nuntiāre, nuntiāvī, nuntiātum	to take a message (11.15)
nūper	recently (64.217)
nupta -ae, f.	wife (17.14)
nympha -ae, f.	nymph (88.6)
Nȳsigena -ae, m.	born on Mount Nysa (64.252)
ō!	oh! (*exclamation*)
obdūrō, obdūrāre, obdūrāvī, obdūrātum	to endure, hold out (8.11–12, 8.19)
oblitterō, oblitterāre, oblitterāvī, oblitterātum	to efface, cause to be forgotten (64.232)
*oblīviscor, oblīviscī, oblītus sum	to forget about (64.208)
obscūrō, obscūrāre, obscūrāvī, obscūrātum	to darken (in colour: 64.227)
obscūrus -a -um	secret, mystical (64.259)
obstinātus -a -um	stubborn, resolute (8.11)
occĭdo, occĭdere, occĭdī, occāsum	to die, fall down (5.4–5)
Ōceanus -ī, m	Oceanus (88.6)
*octo	eight (10.20)
*ōdī, ōdisse	to hate (85.1)
Oetaeus -a -um	of Mount Oeta (62.7)
*offerō, offerre, obtulī, oblātum	to cause, inflict (64.248)
offirmō, offirmāre, offirmāvī, offirmātum	to toughen up, strengthen one's resolve (76.11)
*ōlim	once, a while ago (64.212)
olīva -ae, f.	olive tree (34.8)
olīvum -ī, n.	olive oil (6.8)
Olympus -ī, m.	Olympus (62.1)
omnipotens, omnipotentis	all-powerful (64.171)

*omnis -e	all of (1.6, 5.2, 11.13, 76.9, 76.22), everybody (11.19), everything (17.20, 64.186–7)
*oportet (*impersonal verb*)	it is right, one should (70.4)
*ops, opis, f.	help (34.24, 76.18)
optātus -a -um	longed for (64.141), desirable (62.30)
optingō, optingere, optigī	to fall to one's lot (107.1)
optō, optāre, optāvī, optātum	to wish (40.6, 76.25), to desire (62.42–4, 107.1, 107.8)
ōrāclum -ī, n.	oracle (7.5)
orgia, orgiōrum, n.	mystical objects (64.259), rites (64.260)
*ōs, ōris, n.	mouth (40.5, 64.132)
*ostendō, ostendere, ostendī, ostēnsum	to show (62.7, 64.211)
ostentō, ostentāre, ostentāvī, ostentātum	to hold out the prospect of (64.187)
ōtiōsus -a -um	idle, doing nothing (10.2)
palma -ae, f.	triumph (62.11), palm (of the hand: 64.261)
palūs, palūdis, f.	swamp (17.4, 17.10)
pandō, pandere, pānsum	to display (6.13)
pangō, pangere, pepigī, pāctum	to agree on, settle (62.28)
*pār, păris	fitting, suitable (62.9), well matched (62.57)
parātus -a -um	ready (11.14, 17.2), prepared (76.5)
*parcō, parcere, pepercī	to refrain from (64.146)
*parens, parentis, m.	parent (62.28, 62.58, 62.62, 64.159, 64.210)
*pāreō, pārēre, pāruī, pāritum	to obey (62.61)
*parō, parāre, parāvī, parātum	to get (10.20, 10.30, 10.32), to prepare (40.4, 62.11)
*pars, partis, f.	share (62.63), part, area (64.251)
pars . . . pars . . .	some . . . others (64.256–9)
ex parte	partly (62.62: *see also* 17.18 ex sua parte)
Parthus -a -um	Parthian (11.6)
*passim	everywhere (64.254)
pateō, patēre, patuī	to be available (64.185)

*pater, patris, m.	father (17.13, 62.60–3, 64.180, 64.241)
paternus -a -um	of a father (64.246)
*patior, patī, passus sum	to allow (64.199)
patrius -a -um	ancestral (64.132)
patrōna -ae, f.	protectress (1.9)
patruus -uī, m.	uncle (88.3, 89.3)
*paucus -a -um	few (11.15)
*paulum	for a short time (10.25)
pectus, pectoris, n.	heart (64.125, 64.138, 64.194, 64.198, 64.202, 64.208, 64.221, 76.22)
pecus, pecoris, n.	herd, flock (62.40)
pelagus -ī, n.	sea (64.127, 64.185)
*pellō, pellere, pepulī, pulsum	to drive, beat (64.239)
penetrō, penetrāre, penetrāvī, penetrātum	to penetrate (11.2)
penitus (*adverb*)	deeply, thoroughly (62.14)
pepigēre/pepigērunt *see* pangō	
*per (+ *accusative*)	as far as ... is concerned (10.34), over (17.9)
peraequē (*adverb*)	evenly (6.9)
perditus -a -um	lost (8.2), abandoned (64.177), disastrous, desperate (91.2)
perennis -e	enduring, long-lasting (1.10)
*pereō, perīre, periī/īvī	to be destroyed (8.2), to go to waste (76.9)
perferō, perferre, pertulī, perlātum	to endure (8.11)
perfidus -a -um	deceitful, treacherous (64.132–3, 64.174)
perhibeō, perhibēre, perhibuī, perhibitum	to allege, say (64.124)
periūrium -ī, n.	broken oath (64.135, 64.148)
permulceō, permulcēre, permulsī, permulsum	to caress (64.162)
perniciēs -ēī, f.	disaster (76.20)
pernīciter (*adverb*)	speedily (62.8)
pernumerō, pernumerāre, pernumerāvī, pernumerātum	to count up (7.11)
perpetuus -a -um	everlasting (5.6)

*perveniō, pervenīre, pervēnī, perventum — to reach, get to (40.5)

pervigilō, pervigilāre, pervigilāvī, pervigilātum — to stay awake all night (88.2)

pervincō, pervincere, pervīcī, pervictum — to win through, succeed (76.15)

*pēs, pedis, m. — leg (of a bed 10.22), foot (17.9)

pestis -is, f. — disease (76.20)

*petō, petere, petiī/īvī, petītum — to make for (64.178), strive for (64.241), pursue, court (70.2)

pietās, pietātis, f. — devotion, moral goodness (76.26)

pilī faciō, pilī facere, pilī fēcī, pilī factum — to care a jot for (10.13, 17.17)

pinguis -is — rich (62.3)

pius -a -um — dutiful, devoted (76.2)

*placeō, placēre, placuī (+ dative) — to please (34.21)

plangō, plangere, plānxī, plānctum — to strike, beat (64.261)

*plēnus -a -um (+ ablative) — filled with (89.3)

plūs (adverb) — more (1.10)

*poena -ae, f. — punishment (40.8, 64.192)

polluō, polluere, polluī, pollūtum — to defile (62.46)

pondus -eris, n. — weight (62.51)

*pōns, pōntis, m. — bridge (17.1, 17.5, 17.8, 17.23)

ponticulus -ī, m. (diminutive of pōns) — little bridge (17.3)

pontus -ī, m. — sea (64.179)

*portō, portāre, portāvī, portātum — to carry (64.135)

*portus -ūs, m — port (64.211)

*possum, posse, potuī — to be able

*postquam (conjunction + perfect indicative) — after (11.23, 64.202)

*postrēmus -a -um — last, final (64.191)

*potēns, potēntis — powerful (34.15)

potis, pote — able to (17.24, 76.24), possible (76.16)

*potius (comparative adverb) — rather (64.150)

praeceps, praecipitis — head-first (17.9, 40.2, 64.244)

praeceptum -ī, n. — order (64.159)

*praeda -ae, f. — prey (64.153)

praegestiō, praegestīre — to desire passionately (64.145)

*praemium -ī, n.	reward (64.157)
praeportō, praeportāre	proclaim (64.194)
praeruptus -a -um	sheer, steep (64.126)
praesertim (*adverb*)	especially (10.12)
praestō (+*dative* + sum)	available (64.137)
*praittereā	furthermore, besides (64.184)
praetereō, praeterīre, praeteriī/īvī, praeteritum	to pass by (11.23)
*praetor -ōris, m.	praetor (provincial governor:10.10, 10.13)
prātum -ī, n.	meadow (11.22)
*prīmum (*adverb*)	firstly (64.223)
cum prīmum	as soon as (64.243)
quam prīmum	as soon as possible (64.236)
*prīmus -a -um	first (64.171)
*prior, prius	earlier, former (76.1)
priscus -a -um	old-fashioned (64.159)
*prius (*adverb*)	previously (64.209, 64.238)
* prius . . . quam (*conjunction*)	before (62.29, 64.189–90)
*prō (+ *ablative*)	in return for (64.152, 64.157, 76.26)
probrum -ī, n.	wickedness, disgrace (91.4)
prōcērus -a -um	outstretched, extended (64.261)
prōcurrō, prōcurrere, prōcurrī, prōcursum	to run forwards (64.128)
prōdeō, prōdīre, prōdiī, prōditum	to go forward, advance (88.7)
*prōdo, prōdere, prōdidī, prōditum	to betray, abandon (64.190)
profānus -a -um	uninitiated (64.260)
prōferō, prōferre, prōtulī, prōlātum	to utter, give voice to (64.196)
profundō, profundere, prōfūdī, profūsum	to pour forth (64.202)
profundus -a -um	deep (17.11)
prōgeniēs -ēī, f.	offspring (34.6)
prōmissum -ī, n.	promise (64.139)
*prōmittō, prōmittere, prōmīsī, prōmissum	to promise (64.146)
prōnus -a -um	face down (17.23), downward (62.51)

*prope (*preposition*)   near to (34.7)
prope (*adverb*)   nearly (64.167)
propriē (*adverb*)   truly, fully (107.2)
prōspectō, prōspectāre,   to gaze at (64.249)
   prōspectāvī, prōspectātum
prōspectus -ūs, m.   view (64.241)
prosperus -a -um   successful (64.237)
prōsum, prōdesse, prōfui   to be of benefit (10.8)
prōtendō, prōtendere, prōtendī,   to extend (her gaze: 64.127)
   prōtentum
*prōvincia -ae, f.   province (10.19)
prūriō, prūrīre   to be lustful (88.2)
pudet (*impersonal verb +*   it is shameful, embarrassing (6.5)
   infinitive)
pudīcus -a -um   chaste, faithful (76.24)
*puella -ae, f.   girl (8.3, 8.7, 8.12, 10.16, 10.27, 11.15,
                                             17.14–15, 34.2–4, 62.23, 62.42–7,
                                             89.3)
*puer, puerī, m.   boy (17.12, 34.2–3, 62.42–7)
puerpera -ae, f.   a woman giving birth (34.14)
*pugnō, pugnāre, pugnāvī,   to fight (62.59–60, 62.64)
   pugnātum
pulvīnus -ī, m.   pillow, bolster (6.9)
pulvis, pulveris, m.   dust (64.224)
pūmex, pūmicis, m./f.   pumice-stone (1.2)
puppis -is, f.   stern of a boat, ship (64.172).
pūriter (*adverb*)   righteously (76.19)
purpureus -a -um   purple (64.163)
pūtidus -a -um   foul, stinking (17.10)
*putō, putāre, putāvi, putātum   to think, believe (1.4, 91.3)
quā (*adverb*)   in any way (76.14)
*quaerō, quaerere, quaesiī/īvī,   to ask (7.1), to ask for (76.23), to look
   quaesītum   for, seek out (64.253)
quaesō (+ *imperative*)   please, I ask you (10.25)
*quālis -e   what sort of? (64.177, 64.200, 64.247)
quāliscumque, quālecumque   of whatever sort/quality (1.9)
quālubet (=quā lubet)   no matter how, somehow or other
                                             (40.6)
*quam (+ *adjective*)   how (7.3, 7.7)

after mālō/*comparative*	than (64.151, 70.2)
after prius *see* prius . . . quam	
after tam/tantundem	as (10.32, 17.20)
quam primum *see* primum	
quamvīs	although (91.7)
quandoquidem	since (40.7, 64.218)
quantum (*adverb*)	as much as (8.5, 88.5)
quantumvīs	as much as you like (89.6)
*quantus -a -um	how much? (88.4)
quārē	how? (85.2), why? (76.10, 89.4–6), therefore (1.8, 6.15, 62.17, 64.192, 107.3)
quatiō, quatere, (*no perfect*), quassum	to shake (6.10, 64,256)
*-que	and
quĕō, quīre, quiī/īvī	to be able (64.166)
querella -ae, f.	complaint (64.130, 64.195), lament (64.223)
questus -ūs, m.	complaint (62.36, 64.170)
*quī, quae, quod (*relative pronoun*)	who, what (8.2, 10.9, 10.14, 10.22, 11.22, (=**quis**:17.22), 62.21, 62.27, 62.65, 64.157, 64.180–3, 88.1–3, 89.5, 91.6, etc.)
quī, quae, quod? (*interrogative*)	what sort of? (64.155)
quīcumque, quaecumque, quodcumque	whatever (11.13, 34.21, 76.7, 91.10)
quid?	why? (64.164)
quid esset	how it was (10.6)
quid nī?	how could this not be so? (89.1)
*quīdam, quaedam, quoddam	a certain (17.8)
quīn	why not? (76.11)
*quis? quid?	who, what? (8.16–18, 10.31, 40.3, 40.6, 62.20, 62.24–6, 62.30, 62.37, 88.1–3, 107.7–8)
nescio . . . quid (+ *genitive*)	some sort of (6.4)
nī quid	if not . . . something (6.14)
*quīs = quibus (*from* quī)	(64.145)
quisnam, quaenam, quidnam	who/what, tell me? (10.8, 40.1, 64.154)
*quisquam, quicquam (*pronoun*)	anyone, anything (10.11, 64.168, 76.7, 88.7, 107.1)

*quisquis, quidquid	whoever, whatever (1.8, 6.15)
*quō . . . modo	how (10.7)
*quod	because (64.159, 91.3–5), but (64.228), the fact that (107.4)
quondam	once (8.3, 64.139)
*quoniam	since, seeing that (64.198)
*quoque	also (8.9, 17.22)
*quot	how many? (7.1)
rādix, rādicis, f.	root (62.52)
rapax, rapācis	greedy, ravening (64.156)
rapidus -a -um	fast-running (70.4)
*ratiō -ōnis, f.	good sense (10.29), method, means (64.186)
raucisonus -a -um	raucous (64.263)
Rāvidus -i, m.	Ravidus (40.1)
*recipiō, recipere, recēpī, receptum	to receive (64.248)
reconditus -a -um	secluded, hidden (34.11)
recordor, recordārī, recordātus sum	to recollect, call to mind (76.1)
rector -ōris, m.	ruler (64.204)
*rectus -a -um	standing up straight (10.20)
recumbō, recumbere, recubuī	to sink back, settle (17.4)
*reddō, reddere, reddidī, redditum	to repay (64.157, 64.166, 76.25), to give back (64.217)
*redeō, redīre, rediī, reditum	to return (5.4)
redimiō, redimīre, redimiī, redimītum	to wreathe, encircle (64.193)
redivīvus -a -um	second-hand (17.3)
redūcō, redūcere, redūxī, reductum	to bring back (76.11)
redux, reducis	returning (64.237)
*referō, referre, rettulī, relātum	to bring back (10.11), (with reflexive pronoun: to return: 64.177, 107.5)
religō, religāre, religāvī, religātum	to tie, secure (64.174)
*relinquō, relinquere, relīquī, relictum	to abandon (64.180, 64.200)
rēmus -ī, m.	oar (64.183)
*repente (adverb)	at once (10.3), suddenly (17.24)

requiescō, requiescere, requiēvī, requiētum	to rest (64.176)
requīrō, requīrere, requīsīvī/ requīsiī, requīsītum	to look for (8.13, 62.37), to recall (62.12), to ask (85.1)
*rēs, reī, f.	thing (64.136, 107.7))
resonō, resonāre, resonāvī	to resound, re-echo (11.3)
respectō, respectāre	to expect, await (11.21)
respergō, respergere, respersī, respersum	to spatter (64.181, 64.230)
*respondeō, respondēre, respondī, respōnsum	to reply (10.9, 62.18)
restituō, restituere, restituī, restitūtum	to restore (107.4–5)
*retineō, retinēre, retinuī, retentum	to hold on to, cling to (62.22)
revertor, revertī, reversus sum	to return (62.34)
Rhēnus -ī, m.	Rhine (river: 11.11)
rīsus -ūs, m.	laughter (17.7)
rixa -ae, f.	quarrel (40.4)
*rogō, rogāre, rogāvī, rogātum	to ask out, seek one's company (8.13–14)
Rōmulus -ī, m.	Romulus (34.22)
rudens, rudentis, m.	rope (64.235)
rūmor, rūmōris, m.	gossiping (5.2)
*rumpō, rumpere, rūpī, ruptum	to burst, break (11.20)
rūpēs -is, f.	crag, rock (64.154)
rusticus -a -um	rural (34.19)
sacer, sacra, sacrum	sacred (7.6)
sacrum -ī, n.	religious rite (17.6)
saeclum -ī, n.	generation (1.10)
*saepe	often (62.34, 64.124)
saepiō, saepīre, saepsī, saeptum	to enclose, hedge around (62.39)
*saevus -a -um	harsh (64.159), cruel (64.169, 64.203)
Sagae, Sagārum, m. pl.	The Sagae (a people: 11.6)
sagittiferus -a -um	arrow-wielding (11.6)
sāl, sălis, m.	sea (64.128)
saliō, salīre, saluī/saliī, salitum	to dance, leap (17.2)
Salisubsalus -ī, m.	Salisubsalus (17.6)
saltem (*adverb*)	at least (62.17)

saltus -ūs, m.	glade, glen (34.11)
*salūs -ūtis, f.	safety, well-being (76.15)
sanctus -a -um	holy, blessed (34.22, 64.228), sacred (76.3)
sānē (*adverb*)	certainly (10.4)
*sanguis, sanguinis, m.	blood (64.230)
sapiō, sapere, sapiī/īvī	to be intelligent (17.12)
satiō, satiāre, satiāvī, satiātum	to satisfy (64.147)
*satis	enough (7.2, 7.10, 91.8–9)
saturō, saturāre, saturāvī, saturātum	to satisfy (64.220)
Satyrus -ī, m.	Satyr (64.252)
saucius -a -um	wounded, hurt (64.250)
scelestus -a -um	wretched (8.15)
*scelus, sceleris, n.	wickedness (88.4, 88.7, 91.10)
*sciō, scīre, sciī/īvī, scītum	to know (5.11, 5.13, 88.4)
scopulus -ī, m.	cliff, rock (64.244)
scortillum -ī, n. (*diminutive of scortum*)	little 'tart' (10.3)
scortum -ī, n.	prostitute, 'tart' (6.5)
*scrībō, scrībere, scripsī, scriptum	to write (70.4)
Scylla -ae, f.	Scylla (sea-monster: 64.156)
*sē, suī (*reflexive pronoun*)	himself, herself, itself, themselves
sēcēdō, sēcēdere, sēcessī, sēcessum	to withdraw, slip away (64.189)
sēcrētus -a -um	separate, by itself (62.39)
sector, sectārī, sectātus sum	to pursue (8.10)
sēcum	to themselves (62.12)
*secundus -a -um	second (5.8), favourable, successful (64.222)
secūris -is, f.	axe (17.9)
*sed	but
*sēdēs -is, f.	dwelling, home (64.160, 64.176, 64.229)
*semel (*adverb*)	once (5.5)
*semper	always (62.33)
senecta -ae, f.	old age (64.217)
senescō, senescere, senuī	to grow old (62.56)
*senex, senis, m.	old man (5.2)
sensus -ūs, m.	sense, sensation (64.165, 64.189)

*sentiō, sentīre, sēnsī, sēnsum	to feel (17.20, 85.2)
septemgeminus -a -um	sevenfold (11.7)
sepulcrum -ī, n.	tomb (7.6)
*sequor, sequī, secūtus sum	to follow (64.181)
Serāpis -is/-idis, m.	Serapis (a god: 10.26)
sermō -ōnis, m.	conversation (10.6), words (64.144)
serpens, serpentis, f.	snake (64.258)
serta -ōrum, n. pl.	garlands (6.8)
serva -ae, f.	slave, servant (64.161)
*sēsē = sē	
seu = sīve (11.6)	
sevērus -a -um	strict, unbending (5.2)
*sī	if
sī quis	if anybody/any (76.1, 76.17)
*sīc	thus, in this way (62.8, 62.45, 62.56,
	64.132–4, 64.169, 64.246), on this
	condition (17.5)
sīdus, sīderis, n.	star (7.7, 64.206)
*signum -ī, n.	sign, signal (64.210, 64.222)
Sīlēnus -ī, m.	Silenus (attendant of Bacchus:
	64.252)
*silva -ae, f.	forest (34.10)
*simul (*adverb*)	together, as a group (11.14, 11.18)
* simul ac	as soon as (64.147, 64.233)
simul cum (+ *ablative*)	along with (62.65)
singultus -ūs, m.	sob (64.131)
*sinō, sinere, sīvī, situm	to allow (17.17, 64.222, 88.3)
sistō, sistere, stetī, statum	to set down (64.237)
*sīve . . . sīve . . .	whether . . . or . . . (11.2-9, 76.16)
sodālis -is, m.	friend (10.29)
*sōl, sōlis, m.	the sun (5.4, 8.3, 8.8, 62.41)
solea -ae, f.	horseshoe (17.26)
*soleō, solēre, solitus sum	to be accustomed to (1.3, 34.23)
*sōlus -a -um	alone (62.64, 64.200), solitary
	(64.154), remote (64.184)
sonō, sonāre, sonuī, sonitum	to sound (34.12)
*soror, sorōris, f.	sister (88.1, 89.2)
sospes, sospitis	safe and sound (64.211)
sospitō, sospitāre	to preserve, defend (34.24)

*spērō, spērāre, spērāvī, spērātum	to hope (64.140, 64.180), expect (64.144, 91.1)
*spēs, speī, f.	hope (64.177, 64.186)
spūmō, spūmāre, spūmāvī, spūmātum	to foam, froth (64.155)
stīpendium -iī, n.	tax (64.173)
*stō, stāre, stetī, statum	to stand (17.3)
stolidus -a -um	dull-witted, stupid (17.24)
strīdō, strīdere, strīdī	to screech, scream (64.264)
stupor, stupōris, m.	stupidity (17.21)
*sub (+ ablative)	beneath (64.154)
*subitō	suddenly (76.13)
sublevō, sublevāre, sublevāvī, sublevātum	to stir, raise (17.18)
subrēpō, subrēpere, subrepsī, subreptum	to creep, steal upon (76.21)
*sum, esse, fuī	to be
*summus -a -um	topmost (62.52), the top of (64.241)
super (adverb)	more than enough (7.2, 7.10)
supīnus -a -um	lying flat (17.4), sluggish (17.25)
suppernātus -a -um	hamstrung (17.19)
supplicium -(i)ī, n.	revenge, vengeance (64.203)
suprēmus -a -um	critical, desperate (64.151)
sūra -ae, f.	the lower leg, calf (64.129)
*surgō, surgere, surrēxī, surrēctum	to rise to one's feet (62.3)
*suscipiō, suscipere, suscēpī, susceptum	to undertake (17.6), to take on, incur (88.4–5)
suspendō, suspendere, suspensī, suspensum	to hang up (64.225)
sustollō, sustollere, sustulī, sublātum	to hoist, raise (64.210, 64.235)
*suus -a -um	belonging to oneself (10.1, 11.17, 17.18, 62.45, 62.65, 64.201)
Syrius -a -um	Syrian (6.8)
Syrtis -is, f.	Syrtes (shallows in the sea off Africa: 64.156)
taceō, tacēre, tacuī, tacitum	to be silent (6.3, 6.12, 7.7)
*tacitus -a -um	silent (6.7, 62.37)
taeter, taetra, taetrum	horrible, vile (76.25)

*tālis -e	of such a kind (17.21, 62.59, 64.157, 64.201, 64.214, 64.248)
*tam (+ *adjective/adverb*)	so (6.13, 7.9, 10.18, 89.1–3)
tam ... quam ...	as ... as (10.32)
*tamen	however (10.14, 64.160, 64.188)
*tandem	at last, finally (62.2)
*tangō, tangere, tetigī, tactum	to touch (11.24, 64.172, 89.5)
*tantum -ī, n. (+*partitive genitive*)	such a quantity, so much/many (5.13)
*tantus -a -um	so great (91.9)
tantusdem, tantadem, tantundem	just as much as (17.20)
taurus -ī, m.	bull (64.173, 64.230)
*tectum -ī, n.	barn (34.20), house (64.184, 64.246)
*tēcum	with you (91.7)
tegmen, tegminis, n.	covering (64.129)
*tegō, tegere, texī, tectum	to cover (64.256)
tellūs, tellūris, f.	earth (64.205)
temere (*adverb*)	for nothing (62.9)
temptō, temptāre, temptāvī, temptātum	to attempt, face (11.14)
*tempus, temporis, n.	time (62.3, 62.57, 64.151, 64.169, 64.171)
tenax, tenācis	clinging, sticky (17.26)
tenellulus -a -um	tender, delicate (17.15)
*teneō, tenēre, tenuī, tentum	to hold (11.18), to keep hold of (64.209, 64.238)
tener, tenera, tenerum	delicate, frail (62.51)
tenuis -e	sharp-edged (62.43), slight, faint (64.262), thin (89.1)
teres, teretis	rounded (64.262)
*terra -ae, f.	earth (64.153, 64.224)
*tertius -a -um	third (62.63–4)
Tēthys, Tēthyos, f.	Tethys (sea-goddess: 88.5)
Thēseus, -ei, m. (*accusative*: Thesea)	Theseus (64.133, 64.200, 64.207, 64.239, 64.245, 64.247)
thiasus -ī, m.	worshipping group (64.252)
Thȳas, Thȳados, f.	maenad, bacchant (64.254)
thyrsus -ī, m.	wand, staff (used by Bacchants: 64.256)
tībia -ae, f.	pipe (musical instrument: 64.264)

tinnītus -ūs, m.	ringing sound (64.262)
*tollō, tollere, sustulī, sublātum	to lift up, raise (62.2, 64.129)
torpor, torpōris, m.	sluggishness, lethargy (76.21)
torqueō, torquēre, torsī, tortum	to coil, twist (64.258)
*tōtus -a -um (genitive: tōtius)	all, the whole of (17.10, 62.14, 62.62)
*trādō, trādere, trādidī, trāditum	to hand over, give (62.60)
*trans (preposition + accusative)	over, across (11.9)
*trecentī, -ae, -a	300 (11.18)
tremulus -a -um	shaking (6.10), rocking (17.13), rippling (64.128)
*trēs, tria	three (1.6)
*tristis -e	sad, heartbroken (64.126)
Trivia -ae, f.	Diana (goddess: 34.15)
truculentus -a -um	ferocious, angry (64.179)
*tū, tuī	you (singular)
*tum	then (10.3, 64.126–8, 64.249)
tumulō, tumulāre, tumulāvī, tumulātum	to cover with a burial mound (64.153)
tundō, tundere, tutudī, tūnsum	to beat, buffet (11.4)
tunica -ae, f.	tunic (88.2)
turbō, turbinis, m.	whirlpool (64.149)
turpis -e	vile, disgraceful (91.4)
*tuus, tua, tuum	your
tympanum -ī, n.	tambourine, drum (64.261)
ūdus -a -um	wet (64.131)
*ullus -a -um	any (64.232)
ulmus -ī, f.	elm tree (62.54)
ulna -ae, f.	forearm (17.13)
*ultimus -a -um	furthest away (11.11–12, 88.5), furthest edge of (11.23)
ultrā (adverb)	further (88.7)
*umquam	ever (76.17, 107.1)
unctus -a -um	enriched, well oiled (10.11)
*unda -ae, f.	wave (11.4, 64.128, 64.155, 64.167, 64.185)
*unde	from where (64.127)
*undique	everywhere, in all cases (64.234)
unguis -is, m.	fingernail (62.43)
ūnicus -a -um	one and only (64.215)

*ūnus -a -um	a single (5.3, 5.6, 17.17), one (1.10, 62.32), alone (1.5, 76.15), especial, unique (10.17, 107.7)
*urbs, urbis, f.	city (62.24)
usquam	anywhere (17.20)
*usque	without a break, continuously (5.9)
*ūsus -ūs, m.	familiarity (91.7)
*ut + *subjunctive*	in order that (10.16, 34.9, 40.5, 64.226, 64.230, 64.233, 64.236), with the result that (64.138), that (64.231, 76.23), although (89.5)
*ut + *indicative*	as (10.3, 10.24, 11.21, 17.17, 34.23, 62.49), when (10.5, 64.241), where (11.3, 17.10), like (17.26, 62.39, 76.21), how (62.8, 62.12)
utinam nē	if only ... not (64.171)
*ūtor, ūtī, ūsus sum	to make use of (10.32)
*utrum ... an	whether ... or (10.31, 17.22)
ūva -ae, f.	bunch of grapes (17.16, 62.50)
vacuus -a -um	empty (64.168)
vae	alas for (8.15, 64.196)
vagus -a -um	roaming (64.225)
valēns, valēntis	vigorous (89.2)
*valeō, valēre, valuī, valitum	to thrive (11.17), to be healthy (76.25), to be of use (6.12)
valē!	farewell (8.12)
vanescō, vanescere	to come to nothing (64.199)
varius -a -um	various (10.6)
Vārus -ī, m.	Varus (10.1)
vastus -a -um	dreary, endless (64.127), monstrous (64.156)
vēcors, vēcordis	deranged, frantic (40.4)
*vel	even (17.6)
vēlum -ī, n.	sail (64.235, 64.243)
*velut	just as (11.22, 17.18)
*veniō, venīre, vēnī, ventum	to arrive (10.5, 62.4)
ventitō, ventitāre, ventitāvī, ventitātum	to come and go (8.4)
*ventus -ī, m.	wind (64.142, 64.213, 64.239, 70.4)

venustus -a -um	attractive (89.2)
*vērē (*adverb*)	truly (8.8, 11.19)
*vereor, verērī, veritus sum	to be afraid (17.2)
*vērō	for sure, without fail (64.231)
versō, versāre, versāvī, versātum	to turn, spin (64.149)
versor, versārī, versātus sum	to be busy (64.167)
versus -ūs, m.	verse (6.17)
vertex, verticis, m.	summit (64.244)
vērum	in fact (6.4), but (10.31), but only (17.10), but all the same (76.14)
*vērus -a -um	real, genuine (64.198)
vēsānus -a -um	mad, wild (7.10)
*Vesper, Vesperis, m.	the evening star (62.1)
*vester, vestra, vestrum	your (62.17, 64.160)
vestīgium -(i)ī, n.	foot (64.162)
*vestis -is, f.	coverlet, bedspread (64.163), cloth (64.234)
*vestrum = *genitive of* vōs	
veternus -i, m.	sloth (17.24)
*vetus, veteris	old (7.6, 10.22)
*victōria -ae, f.	victory (62.16)
viden = *videsne?* (62.8)	
*videō, vidēre, vīdī, vīsum	to see (7.8, 8.2, 10.2, 17.21, 62.8, 91.5)
*videor, vidērī, vīsus sum	to seem, appear (8.16) to be obvious (10.3)
viduus -a -um	single, celibate (6.6, 62.49)
vigeō, vigēre, viguī	to stay fresh (64.232)
vigilō, vigilāre, vigilāvī, vigilātum	to stay awake (62.33)
*vincō, vincere, vīcī, victum	to defeat (62.9, 62.16)
vindex, vindicis, m.	avenging (64.192)
violō, violāre, violāvī, violātum	to violate, break (76.3)
*vir, virī, m.	man (62.28, 62.58, 64.143–4, 64.192)
vireō, virēre, viruī	to be green, lush (34.10)
virginitās, virginitātis, f.	virginity (62.62)
virgō, virginis, f.	unmarried woman (1.9, 62.45, 62.56), bride (62.4, 62.59)
viridis -e	fresh (17.14)
*virtūs, virtūtis, f.	courage (64.218)
vīsō, vīsere, vīsī	to go to see (11.10, 64.211)

*vīta -ae, f.	life (8.15, 64.157, 64.215, 76.19, 107.8)
vītis -is, f.	grapevine (62.49)
*vīvō, vīvere, vīxī, vīctum	to live (5.1, 11.17, 107.7), to spend your life being (8.10, 10.33), to be (89.2)
*vix tandem	only just, after all this time (62.2)
*vocō, vocāre, vocāvī, vocātum	to call, summon (6.17)
volitō, volitāre, volitāvī, volitātum	to hurry in flight (64.251)
*volō, velle, voluī	to be willing (6.3, 64.138, 76.24), to want (6.16, 8.7, 10.26, 17.8, 17.23, 40.6, 40.8)
voluntās, voluntātis, f.	will (11.13)
voluptās, voluptātis, f.	pleasure (76.1)
volvō, volvere, volvī, volūtum	to turn over (64.250)
vorāgō, vorāginis, f.	abyss (17.11), quagmire (17.26)
vorō, vorāre, vorāvī, vorātum	to swallow (88.8)
*vōs, vestrum/vestrī	you (*plural*) (64.199, 76.17)
*vōx, vōcis, f.	utterance (64.125, 64.166, 64.202), voice (64.140)
vulgus -ī, n.	general public, mob (40.5)